Developing Life Skills

by
DEBBIE RADLIFF

COPYRIGHT © 1999 Mark Twain Media, Inc.

ISBN 1–58037–115–9

Printing No. CD-1339

Mark Twain Media, Inc., Publishers
Distributed by Carson-Dellosa Publishing Company, Inc.

Table Of Contents

Understanding Yourself

Self-Analysis

You are a very special person! Each person is unique. **Unique** means that no other person on this planet is exactly like you! What makes you unique? Your appearance, personality, and skills are all things that make you different from anyone else.

An important part of you is your personality. **Personality** is the total of all the behavioral qualities that make up an individual. Personality includes the way you feel, think, speak, dress, and relate to other people. You have many personality traits that make you unique. **Traits** are the qualities that make you different from other people. Some traits are considered more desirable to have than others. Here are some examples of traits:

kind	depressed	quiet	loud
friendly	happy	excitable	responsible
sloppy	nice	cooperative	confident
moody	funny	lazy	well-mannered

There are hundreds of other traits! Can you list more? The combination of your traits makes your unique personality!

You need to understand who you are so you can feel good about yourself. Understanding who you are is called **self-analysis**. How you feel about yourself is called **self-concept**. Learning about yourself can help you develop a positive self-concept. We all have many good traits, but nobody is perfect. If you have some traits that you want to improve, you can do it! Learn more about your personality and feel good about yourself. You are a unique and special person!

Additional Activities:

1. Discuss the following:
   a. What traits do you want your friends to have?
   b. What makes you feel happy?
   c. What makes you feel proud?

2. Write a positive trait for each person in the class. Go around the room and ask each person to stand while the others read the positive comments about him/her.

3. Construct a collage of magazine pictures and phrases showing things that you enjoy.

Name: _____ Date: _____

For the Student

1. What is the definition of unique?

_____

_____

2. Define personality.

_____

_____

3. What are traits?

_____

_____

4. List ten traits.

_____

_____

_____

_____

5. What does self-analysis mean?

_____

_____

6. What does self-concept mean?

_____

_____

7. List five desirable traits.

     a. _____

     b. _____

     c. _____

     d. _____

     e. _____

8. List five undesirable traits.

     a. _____

     b. _____

     c. _____

     d. _____

     e. _____

Name: _____ Date: _____

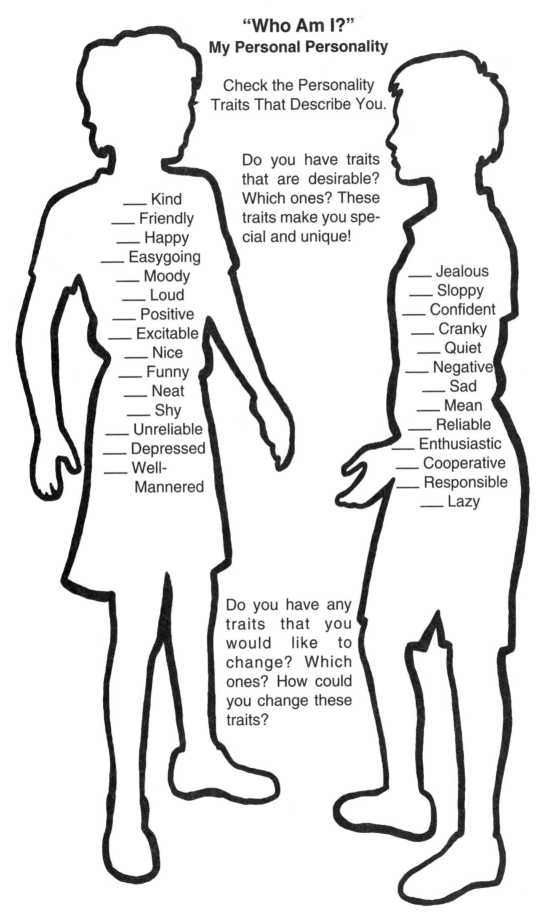

"Who Am I?"
My Personal Personality

Check the Personality Traits That Describe You.

Do you have traits that are desirable? Which ones? These traits make you special and unique!

___ Kind
___ Friendly
___ Happy
___ Easygoing
___ Moody
___ Loud
___ Positive
___ Excitable
___ Nice
___ Funny
___ Neat
___ Shy
___ Unreliable
___ Depressed
___ Well-Mannered

___ Jealous
___ Sloppy
___ Confident
___ Cranky
___ Quiet
___ Negative
___ Sad
___ Mean
___ Reliable
___ Enthusiastic
___ Cooperative
___ Responsible
___ Lazy

Do you have any traits that you would like to change? Which ones? How could you change these traits?

Name: _____ Date: _____

For the Student: My Self-Concept

Finish the following statements.

1. I am proud of myself when I

_____

_____

2. I am happy when I

_____

_____

3. Activities that I enjoy are

_____

_____

4. I feel successful when I

_____

_____

5. I feel helpful when I

_____

_____

6. I love to

_____

_____

7. I cherish my

_____

_____

8. My most prized possession is

_____

_____

9. My best personality traits are

_____

_____

10. I am skilled at

_____

_____

Setting Goals

A **goal** is something you want to accomplish. You will set many goals in your lifetime. You will set short-term goals and long-term goals.

Short-term goals are goals that can be met in a short amount of time. Some examples of short-term goals are:
- clean your room this week.
- complete your book report by Friday.
- save $25.00 for Christmas presents.

Long-term goals are goals that are met over a long period of time. Some examples of long-term goals are:
- get a college degree.
- save money to buy a new bike this summer.
- get married and have children.

Each goal should answer these three questions:
- What are you going to do?
- How are you going to do it?
- When are you going to do it?

Setting goals can help you accomplish many things in your life. Try to set goals that are realistic, but still a challenge. **If you try, you can do anything!!!**

Additional Activities:

1. Discuss the following:
   a. What is your career goal for the future?
   b. What is your housing goal for the future?
   c. If you won a thousand dollars, how would you spend it? Why?

2. Interview a person presently working in the career you hope to have in the future. Ask the following questions (plus some of your own!):
   a. What are the educational requirements for the job?
   b. What skills are required to perform the job?
   c. How many years will it take to be trained for the job?
   d. What is the beginning salary for the job?

3. Have each student write a long-term goal on a sheet of white paper. Share the goals with the class. After students decorate the pages with pictures and/or stickers that emphasize the goal, post the goals in the classroom.

Name: _____   Date: _____

For the Student

1. What is a goal?

_____

_____

2. What is a short-term goal?

_____

_____

3. List three of your short-term goals.

     a. _____

     b. _____

     c. _____

4. What is a long-term goal?

_____

_____

5. List three of your long-term goals.

     a. _____

     b. _____

     c. _____

6. What are the three questions each goal should answer?

     a. _____

     b. _____

     c. _____

7. State a short-term goal that you can reach today.

_____

_____

8. How will you reach this goal?

_____

_____

9. When will you reach this goal?

_____

_____

10. Why is this goal important to you?

_____

_____

_____

Making Decisions/Solving Problems

A **decision** is a choice. You make lots of decisions every day. Some decisions require a lot of thought. Others require little or no thought. Let's look at a few of the decisions you make each day:

- What time will you wake up?
- What will you wear to school?
- What will you eat for breakfast?
- Will you pack your lunch or eat the hot lunch at school?
- Will you ride the bus, walk, or ride your bike to school?
- Who will you sit with if you ride the bus?
- Which book will you choose for your book report?

Did you realize that you make so many decisions in just a few hours of your day? Many of your decisions or choices are made without even thinking about them. Most of these decisions are not really that important. What you wear to school probably will not make much difference in your life or anyone else's. These are simple everyday decisions and choices.

Some decisions are much more important. They may have a greater impact on your life. They may involve relationships with family and friends or how you spend your time or money. Many decisions involve solving a problem. These decisions require much more thought. Some of these decisions are:

- Which bike will you buy?
- How will you earn the money to buy the bike?
- Will you baby-sit or go to the dance on Friday?
- Where will your family go on vacation?
- Which clubs will you join?

Decision making can help you reach all of your short-term and long-term goals. You will be making decisions every day for the rest of your life!! There is a step-by-step process that can make decision making easier. The same process can also be used to solve problems. It can help you solve tiny problems or huge problems. The steps in decision making and problem solving are as follows.

1. STATE THE DECISION OR DEFINE THE PROBLEM.
Some decisions involve just making a choice. Others involve solving a problem. State your decision in the form of a goal.

2. LIST ALL OF THE POSSIBLE ALTERNATIVES AND GATHER INFORMATION.
List all of the possible ways you might reach your goal. Try to list two or more possible alternatives. Gather any information that you need to help you make your decision.

3. EXPLORE EACH ALTERNATIVE.

Think about the pros and cons of each alternative. Think about what would happen if you chose each alternative.

4. CHOOSE THE BEST ALTERNATIVE.

Select the alternative that will help you reach your goal in the best way. Make a decision.

5. TAKE ACTION.

This can be the most difficult part of the process. You must do what is necessary to reach your goal.

6. EVALUATE YOUR DECISION.

Decide if your decision helped you reach your goal. Did you make a good decision?

NOW GET READY TO MAKE YOUR NEXT DECISION OR SOLVE YOUR NEXT PROBLEM!

Additional Activities:

1. Make a list of all the decisions you make in one day. Which of the decisions required a lot of thought?

2. Write a problem on an index card. Read the problem to the class. Discuss possible solutions to the problem.

3. Solve these problems using the decision-making process. Share your solution with the class.

    a.   John is getting a C in science and wants to raise the grade to a B. How can he achieve this?

    b.   Cathy wants to earn money to buy a new pair of in-line skates. How can she earn the money?

    c.   Sue has been arguing with her younger sister a lot lately. How can she get along better with her sister?

Name: _____ Date: _____

For the Student

Select a decision to make or a problem to solve. Work through the process to make your choice or solve your problem.

1. State your decision or problem in the form of a goal.

_____

_____

_____

2. List three possible alternatives and gather information to help you reach your goal.

_____

_____

_____

_____

3. Explore each alternative.

_____

_____

_____

_____

_____

_____

_____

_____

_____

4. Choose the best alternative. Make a decision.

_____

_____

_____

5. Take action.

_____

_____

_____

6. Evaluate your decision.

_____

_____

_____

Communicating

Your day is filled with many kinds of communication. **Communication** is the exchange of information. It includes sending information and receiving it. Communication can occur many different ways. You communicate when you speak, listen, read, and write. Communicating is a part of almost everything you do!!

Research shows that people spend 70 percent of each day communicating in some way! People spend 42 percent of that communication listening, 32 percent speaking, 15 percent reading, and 11 percent writing. Since you spend so much of your day communicating, it is very important that you become a skilled communicator!

There are two main types of communication: verbal communication and nonverbal communication. **Verbal communication** is the use of words to send information. Speaking and writing are ways to send verbal communications. Listening and reading are ways to receive verbal communications.

Nonverbal communication is any means of sending a message that does not use words. Have you heard the term "body language"? **Body language** is a form of nonverbal communication by sending messages through body movements. These movements include gestures, posture, and facial expressions. Other forms of nonverbal communication are your appearance, grooming, and reactions. You can send a message in many instances without making a sound. Sometimes the message you send may be incorrect or misunderstood! Being aware of forms of nonverbal communication will help you send the correct message to other people.

Let's take a closer look at the methods of communication.

VERBAL COMMUNICATION

1. **Listening.** Being a good listener is very important. To be a good listener, you should:
   - pay attention.
   - act interested.
   - maintain eye contact.
   - be patient.
   - stay focused.
   - ask questions if you do not understand.
   - listen to the way the speaker uses his/her voice.

2. **Speaking.** Good speaking skills are important also. A good speaker should:
   - keep messages short and to the point.
   - be considerate to others.
   - respect the listeners.
   - use language and pronunciations clearly.
   - use voice to emphasize the message.
   - maintain eye contact.

3. **Reading.** Reading is receiving information through the written word. Reading is used to learn information and for enjoyment. We receive a lot of information by reading textbooks, newspapers, magazines, and letters.

4. **Writing.** Writing is sending information through the written word. You write homework assignments, letters, answer test questions, and keep a journal or diary. Many jobs require writing reports or business letters. It is important to have good writing skills. To be a good writer:
- messages should be clear and easy to understand.
- handwriting should be legible.
- spelling and grammar should be correct.

NONVERBAL COMMUNICATION

1. **Appearance.** Appearance is very important. Your appearance is the first impression a person receives. If the first impression turns people off, you may lose the chance to get a job or make a new friend. You do not have to be pretty or attractive to have a good appearance. If you are dressed appropriately and are well-groomed, you will send a positive message. **Grooming** is caring for your body. Being well-groomed means your clothes, hair, teeth, and nails are clean and neat. Your clothes should be appropriate for the situation. The clothing you wear to school would be different from the clothes you wear to a job interview. A neat and clean appearance will send a positive message to the people you meet.

2. **Body Language.** Body language sends a message through body movements. It can send positive or negative messages. It includes:
- facial expressions: smiles, frowns, etc.
- gestures: waves, thumbs up, etc.
- posture: slumping, dragging feet, etc.
- manners: polite behavior.

THINK ABOUT THE VERBAL AND NONVERBAL MESSAGES YOU SEND. BE A GOOD COMMUNICATOR!

Additional Activities:

1. Cut out pictures from magazines to communicate the following nonverbal messages:

surprise	fear	happiness
anger	boredom	confusion
love	interest	enthusiasm

Name: _____ Date: _____

For the Student

1. Communication means:

_____

_____

2. State the two main types of communication and examples of each.

a. _____

_____

_____

b. _____

_____

_____

3. List five characteristics of a good listener.

a. _____

b. _____

c. _____

d. _____

e. _____

4. List five characteristics of a good speaker.

a. _____

b. _____

c. _____

d. _____

e. _____

5. List three ways that you receive written information.

a. _____

b. _____

c. _____

6. List three ways that you send written information.

a. _____

b. _____

c. _____

7. What is body language?

_____

_____

_____

Name: _____ Date: _____

8. What is grooming?

_____

_____

9. Give four examples of negative body language.

a. _____

b. _____

c. _____

d. _____

10. Give four examples of positive body language.

a. _____

b. _____

c. _____

d. _____

11. Place a **+** by the characteristics of a positive message or communication technique.
    Place a **-** by the characteristics of a negative message or communication technique.

___ a. thumbs down   ___ n. wrinkled clothing

___ b. straight posture   ___ o. clear speech

___ c. paying attention   ___ p. smile

___ d. eye contact   ___ q. good manners

___ e. handshake   ___ r. focus on the topic

___ f. frown   ___ s. thumbs up

___ g. negative attitude   ___ t. raised eyebrows

___ h. messy hair   ___ u. hug

___ i. pat on the back   ___ v. slumped shoulders

___ j. mumbling   ___ w. dirty fingernails

___ k. wave   ___ x. positive attitude

___ l. bounce in your step   ___ y. avoiding eye contact

___ m. neat appearance

Relationships

Friends

Everyone likes to have friends. Friends are people who care about you and share your interests. We have many types of friendships. The different types of friendships are acquaintances, casual friends, and close friends.

Acquaintances are people that you have met, but do not know well. Most of us have lots of acquaintances. They may go to your church, school, or live near you.

Casual friends are people that share the same interests and activities. We have lots of casual friends in our classes, school activities, and sports teams.

Close friends are your best friends. You spend most of your time with your close friends. You feel comfortable telling them your private thoughts and secrets.

You have many friends now and will get many more throughout your lifetime. Some friendships last forever, while others last only a short time. Your friends may change as you grow older and develop different interests.

How do you choose your friends? Most of us want friends who have good qualities. Some important qualities for a friend are:

loyalty: Friends who will be your friend no matter what. They stand by you in good times and bad times.

caring: Friends who care about your feelings and want the best for you.

reliability: Friends who you can count on. If they tell you they will do something, you know they will keep their promise.

trustworthiness: Friends who can keep a secret. If you tell your friend a secret, he or she will not tell anyone else!

Do you have these qualities? Are you a good friend? What qualities do you want your friends to have? Some people make new friends easily. Others have a hard time making new friends. Some tips for meeting people are:

- get involved in many activities—join teams and clubs.
- talk to the people you meet—introduce yourself and start a conversation.
- have a positive attitude—people like to be around someone friendly and fun.

Try to enlarge your circle of friends. Making new friends is fun!

Additional Activities

1. Discuss qualities to look for in a friend.

2. Discuss ways to make new friends.

3. Discuss reasons for ending a friendship.

Name: _____ Date: _____

For the Student

1. An acquaintance is

_____

_____

2. List three places you might meet acquaintances.

   a. _____

   b. _____

   c. _____

3. Casual friends are

_____

_____

4. List three places you might meet casual friends.

   a. _____

   b. _____

   c. _____

5. Close friends are

_____

_____

6. List six qualities you want your friends to have.

   a. _____

   b. _____

   c. _____

   d. _____

   e. _____

   f. _____

7. How do you pick a best friend?

_____

_____

_____

8. Give an example of a friend who is:

   a. loyal: _____

   b. caring: _____

   c. reliable: _____

   d. trustworthy: _____

Family

Your family is one of the most important parts of your life! A **family** is a group of people who are related to each other. Family members may be related by birth, marriage, or adoption. Families come in many sizes and combinations. The different family types are listed below.

Nuclear family: A nuclear family is formed when a man and a woman with no children marry. After the marriage, they may choose to have children or adopt children. These children are part of their nuclear family.

Single-parent family: A single-parent family occurs when only one parent raises the children. It may be the father or the mother. A single-parent family occurs when parents divorce, when one parent dies, or when the parents do not marry.

Blended family: A blended family is formed when the parent in a single-parent family marries another single person or a single parent.

Extended family: An extended family is the family and all of the relatives. It includes parents, children, grandparents, brothers, sisters, aunts, uncles, cousins, nieces, nephews, and in-laws. The extended family may live in the same home, near each other, or be spread over great distances.

Family members must work together to produce a healthy, happy, family. Members of the family need to share responsibilities. Responsibilities change as the family members grow older. What are your responsibilities in your family? Are you the family dishwasher, garbage person, housekeeper, baby-sitter, or cook?

Family members need to spend quality time together. Quality time is spent enjoying the company of others. Your family may spend quality time talking, playing games, traveling, or just hanging out. Spending time together as a family helps to strengthen the family relationships.

You can strengthen your family relationships by:
- spending time together.
- communicating with family members.
- showing appreciation and respect for each other.
- sharing values and beliefs.
- resolving conflicts.
- coping with conflicts.

Each family changes over a period of years. These changes are stages in the family life cycle. The **family life cycle** includes all the changes that occur in a family over a period of many years. The stages in the family life cycle are listed below.

The beginning stage occurs when a couple gets married and establishes a home together. They must learn to get along with each other and manage a household.

The expanding stage is when the couple has children. This stage continues until all of the couple's children are born. It involves learning to become a parent. It includes managing demands on time, money, and responsibility.

The developing stage occurs when the children enter school. It is a busy time for the family with many school activities. This stage continues until the first child leaves home.

The launching stage occurs when the children leave home for college, marriage, or other reasons. It is a time when parents will need to adjust to having no children around. The parents may use this time to travel and find new interests to fill the void.

The aging stage happens when the parents retire from their jobs. If they have good health, they may travel and enjoy their retirement years.

Sometimes a family may be in two stages at the same time. Each stage provides different demands for time, money, and living space.

Each family is unique. It is your responsibility to be a good family member. Cherish your family, it is an important part of your life!!

Additional Activities:

1. Discuss the way your family celebrates holidays, birthdays, and other special occasions. What are some of your family's traditions at these celebrations? Why are these celebrations important to you?

2. Make a collage of pictures that show your family spending time together. Share the collage with the class.

3. Write a short story depicting all of the stages in the family life cycle.

4. Collect magazine pictures of families in the different stages of the family cycle. Share them with the class.

5. Draw a poster depicting the family life cycle.

6. Discuss the responsibilities for the following members of your family:
   mother:
   father:
   siblings:
   you:
   Will you have additional responsibilities as you get older? What will they be?

7. Discuss ways to resolve family conflicts.

8. Discuss ways to show care for family members.

9. Draw a family tree listing family members as far back as you can. Provide pictures of the family members if available. Display the family trees in the class. Share interesting stories about your family with the class.

Name: _____ Date: _____

For the Student

1. Match each word with the correct meaning.

___ single-parent family
___ beginning stage
___ extended family
___ developing stage
___ family life cycle
___ expanding stage
___ family
___ aging stage
___ nuclear family
___ launching stage
___ blended family

a. parents and their children
b. begins when a couple has children and continues until the children begin school
c. the children begin to leave home
d. a group of people related to each other
e. a family has school-age children
f. two families that are joined together by the marriage of parents
g. the stages of change in a family over a period of years
h. the family and all of its relatives
i. when a couple gets married and establishes a home together
j. the parents retire and grow older
k. one parent raises the family

2. Read each of the following family situations and decide which type of family is represented in each situation. Write the family type in the blank. Your choices are **nuclear**, **single-parent**, **blended**, and **extended family**.

_____ a. Mary had two children from a previous marriage. John had one child from a previous marriage. Mary and John married and bought a large house for their new family.

_____ b. Terry and Joe got married five years ago. They recently adopted a three-year-old boy and a baby girl. They are really enjoying their growing family.

_____ c. Christy lives with her parents and two brothers. Her grandmother died recently, leaving her grandfather alone, so he now lives with them. They are really enjoying their growing family.

_____ d. Chad's parents recently divorced. He lives with his mother, but visits his father on the weekends.

3. Why is your family important to you?

_____

_____

Name: _____ Date: _____

4. List five ways to strengthen your family relationships.

    a. _____

    b. _____

    c. _____

    d. _____

    e. _____

5. How does your family resolve conflicts?

_____

_____

6. Give an example of a family in each stage of the family life cycle.

    a. The beginning stage: _____

_____

_____

    b. The expanding stage: _____

_____

_____

    c. The developing stage: _____

_____

_____

    d. The launching stage: _____

_____

_____

    e. The aging stage: _____

_____

_____

7. Which of the stages do you think will be the most expensive for the family? _____

    Why? _____

_____

8. Which stage will allow the parents to have the most free time? _____

    Why? _____

_____

9. Which stage will be the busiest time for the family? _____

    Why? _____

_____

10. Which stage of the family life cycle is your family in right now? _____

_____

Caring for Children

You are getting old enough to begin baby-sitting. Baby-sitting is fun and a great way to earn money! Caring for children is a huge responsibility, however. Are you ready for this responsibility?

When you are responsible for a child, you must keep him or her safe and free from danger. You must watch the child at all times to keep him or her from getting hurt. Some ways to keep children safe are:

- Use straps on high chairs and strollers to keep the baby from falling or climbing out.
- Use child gates to block stairways and avoid falls.
- Keep screens on windows to prevent falls.
- Use a playpen to keep children safe when you are busy. Place safe toys in the playpen.
- Keep plastic bags away from children. They can place them over their heads and suffocate.
- Do not leave children unsupervised around water, even the bathtub! Children can drown in less than an inch of water.
- Cover the electrical outlets with child-proof plugs to prevent shock if the child places something in the outlet.
- Keep hot things out of reach.
- Keep small and sharp things out of reach so that the child will not get choked or cut.
- Keep the doors locked, and do not allow strangers into the house.
- Keep children away from traffic.
- Keep medicines and poisons out of reach.
- Never leave a small child unattended.

Accidents can still happen even if you are very careful. Knowing first aid for minor accidents is very helpful. In case of a real emergency, you must know what to do. Ask the parents to leave a phone number where they or a relative can be reached in case of an emergency. Know emergency numbers for the police, ambulance, and fire department. Also know the address and phone number of the house where you are baby-sitting. Stay calm and get help quickly.

A baby sitter needs a bag of tricks to keep children happy. Bringing some age-appropriate toys or games with you can be fun for both you and the child. Do not worry, most children have plenty of their own toys if you do not bring any. Be willing to entertain the children. That is what you are being paid to do! If you are a fun and good baby sitter, chances are that you will have lots more baby-sitting jobs in the future.

Ask the parents what rules and routine or schedule they want the children to follow. Some good things to ask about are:

- appropriate food and/or snacks.
- appropriate activities (certain games, indoors, outdoors, etc.).
- bedtime (maybe bath-time, etc.).
- telephone rules.
- television rules.

A good baby sitter should:
- follow the parents' directions.
- be reliable.
- write down telephone messages for the parents.
- play with the children.
- keep appointments and be on time.
- keep the children safe.
- leave the house as neat as it was when you arrived.
- tell the parents about any problems or accidents.
- be a good role model for the children.

Baby-sitting is good practice for becoming a parent in the future. Make your baby-sitting experiences fun and safe for yourself and the children under your care.

Additional Activities:

1. Discuss appropriate activities and games for babies, toddlers, preschoolers, and school age children.

2. Create a bag of tricks containing toys and games for children of various ages to take with you on your baby-sitting jobs.

3. Discuss how to handle the following emergencies:
    a. scraped knee
    b. splinters
    c. fire
    d. choking
    e. deep cut

4. Discuss the characteristics and behaviors of a bad baby sitter.

5. Role-play the following situations.
    a. Trying to comfort a toddler who misses his mommy
    b. Trying to get a baby to stop crying
    c. Trying to get a second-grader to go to bed
    d. Answering the door to a stranger
    e. The child you are caring for breaks a vase
    f. Breaking up a fight between two siblings in your care
    g. The child you are caring for fell and you think his arm may be broken
    h. A bad storm develops and the tornado siren is sounding

Name: _____ Date: _____

For the Student

1. List 10 ways to keep the children you are caring for safe.

_____

_____

_____

_____

_____

2. List five pieces of information you should have in case of an emergency.

_____

_____

_____

3. What is the most important role of a baby-sitter?

_____

_____

4. How could you comfort a toddler who misses his or her mommy?

_____

_____

5. What information should you get from the parents before they leave home?

_____

_____

6. What should you do if you have to cancel a baby-sitting appointment?

_____

_____

7. List five characteristics of a good baby sitter.

_____

_____

_____

_____

8. List five examples of being a good role model for the children.

_____

_____

_____

_____

Caring for the Elderly

We all grow old! Right now it is probably hard for you to imagine getting old! Do you have older grandparents or relatives? Have you seen changes in their appearances and abilities over the past years? Aging brings change. Some of the changes are good and others are not so good. These changes usually happen gradually over many years. Some physical changes associated with aging are in the list below.

- wrinkling skin
- change in hair color
- hearing loss
- change in posture
- vision changes

- arthritis
- dental problems
- changes in sense of taste
- increased health problems
- forgetting things

Some people experience more difficulties associated with aging than others. People age at different rates. One person aged 75 may still live alone, cook for himself, and walk a mile a day. Another person the same age may be confined to a wheel chair and live in a nursing home. Everyone's abilities are different.

Many of the problems associated with aging can be solved, or at least made better. Some people can hear better with the help of a hearing aid. Special attachments can be added to a phone to amplify the sound. Magnifying glasses can be used to enlarge print. Many books are available in large print, too. We need to be aware of the problems associated with aging and try to make life easier for our elderly friends and relatives.

All of the changes associated with aging are not bad. Many elderly people are retired from their jobs. They have more time to enjoy hobbies and spending time with their families. They also have more time to travel. Many elderly people enjoy retirement if they are healthy and able to remain active. Many elderly people volunteer at hospitals and day care centers. They can contribute a lot to help others.

We can be helpful to our elderly friends and relatives. We can also learn a lot about life from their experiences. It is a great experience to spend time and learn from an elderly friend or relative. You will gain knowledge and they will probably love the company!

Additional Activities:

1. Discuss solutions to help an elderly person who is experiencing problems with vision, hearing, or arthritis.

2. Interview an elderly friend or relative. Ask them questions about their life when they were your age. Ask about problems related to aging. Share your findings with your classmates.

3. Visit a nursing home and talk to the people living there. Help them by reading to them, writing letters for them, or just listening.

Name: _____ Date: _____

For the Student

1. List six physical changes that usually occur during the aging process.

   a. _____

   b. _____

   c. _____

   d. _____

   e. _____

   f. _____

2. Explain ways you help an elderly person experiencing a hearing loss.

   _____

   _____

3. How could you help an elderly friend with vision problems?

   _____

   _____

4. List three good things and three bad things about growing old.

   _____

   _____

   _____

   _____

5. List three ways you can help an elderly acquaintance.

   _____

   _____

   _____

6. List three ways an elderly person can help others.

   _____

   _____

   _____

7. List three housing alternatives for the elderly.

   _____

   _____

   _____

8. What would you like to do when you become elderly?

   _____

   _____

   _____

Consumer Skills

Money Management

Money plays an important part in your life. It can bring you pleasure when you buy something you want. It can bring you worry or trouble if you do not have enough to pay your bills or meet your needs. You must learn to manage your money to get the most from it! You need to form a budget to manage your money wisely.

A **budget** is a spending plan to help you manage your money. It includes money for needs and wants. **Needs** are items that you are unable to live without. Some examples of needs are food, clothing, and shelter. **Wants** are items that you desire, but can live without. They are items that you would like to own for pleasure or entertainment. Some examples of wants are clothes for special occasions, snacks, going to movies, and vacations. You should spend money to meet your needs before you spend it on your wants!

You can use your decision-making skills to help you spend your money wisely. You need to set goals for how you will spend your money. Short-term and long-term goals are the things you want to purchase or achieve with your money. **Short-term goals** are the things you want to purchase in a year or less. **Long-term goals** are things that you want to spend your money on several years from now. You may want to prioritize your goals. **Prioritize** means to rank them in order of importance. The most important goal would be number one.

To plan a budget, first you need to estimate your income. **Income** is all of the money that is available for your spending. List all of your sources of income. Include allowance, wages, gifts, and interest.

Next, you need to estimate your expenses. Expenses are divided into two categories. Fixed **expenses** are paid on a regular basis and in a set amount. Some fixed expenses that you might have now are payments for a bicycle, dues for a club, or school lunches. In the future, your expenses might include rent, house payment, utilities (water, electricity, etc.), insurance, and loan payments. **Flexible expenses** are less regular and vary in amounts. Some examples of flexible expenses are food, clothing, recreation, and gifts.

The amount of your income should be greater than your expenses. If your expenses are greater than your income, you will be in debt.

You need to save some of your income to meet your short-term and long-term spending goals. It is a good idea to set up a savings account at your local bank. Saving money regularly each month is a good routine to follow. This money will earn interest each month and the amount will grow.

Following a budget will help you see where your money goes each month. It will teach you how to make wise spending decisions so you can meet your spending goals.

Additional Activity:

Keep a record of all the money you spend for one week. List date, item, and amount spent. Discuss your spending with the class. Discuss amounts spent on needs and wants.

Name: _____ Date: _____

For the Student

1. What is a budget?

_____

_____

2. How can money bring you pleasure?

_____

_____

3. How can money bring you worry or trouble?

_____

_____

4. List four examples of needs and wants.

Needs   Wants

a. _____   a. _____

b. _____   b. _____

c. _____   c. _____

d. _____   d. _____

5. List three examples of short-term spending goals.

a. _____

b. _____

c. _____

6. List three examples of long-term spending goals.

a. _____

b. _____

c. _____

7. List three forms of income.

a. _____

b. _____

c. _____

8. List three examples of fixed and flexible expenses.

Fixed Expenses   Flexible Expenses

a. _____   a. _____

b. _____   b. _____

c. _____   c. _____

9. Why is it important to save money regularly?

_____

_____

Name: _____ Date: _____

For the Student

My Weekly Budget

Budget for the week of _____ to _____ .

INCOME		EXPENSES	
Source	**Amount**	**Fixed Expenses**	**Amount**
_____	_____	_____	_____
_____	_____	_____	_____
_____	_____	_____	_____
_____	_____	_____	_____
_____	_____	_____	_____
_____	_____	_____	_____
_____	_____		

		Flexible Expenses	**Amount**
		_____	_____
		_____	_____
		_____	_____
		_____	_____
		_____	_____
		_____	_____
		_____	_____

TOTAL INCOME _____   **TOTAL EXPENSES** _____

TOTAL INCOME _____
TOTAL EXPENSES _____

SAVINGS _____

Evaluate your spending. Was your budget successful? How can you save more money?

Smart Shopping

You work hard to earn your money, so you should spend it wisely. You can make wise spending decisions by being an informed shopper. Consider the following when you need to purchase goods or services:

WHETHER TO BUY: Do you really need this item? Is it a quality item?

WHEN TO BUY: Try to make purchases when items are on sale. The best sales are usually at the end of the season. Purchase your camping supplies for next year in August or September. Purchase wrapping paper right after the holiday season. Stock up on items you use often when they are on sale. Many stores have good sales around the holidays. Watch your newspaper for sale ads. Using coupons can save you money too!

WHERE TO BUY: There are many different types of stores. Large towns offer more stores to pick from than small communities. Some stores have cheaper prices and better sales than others. Large discount stores and outlet stores usually have the lowest prices. Small specialty stores and boutiques normally have higher prices, but may offer great service and sales. Check out the stores in your town to learn where to purchase various items.

PLAN AHEAD: Think about what you need to buy before you shop. Make a list and follow it to avoid impulse buying. **Impulse buying** is buying an item without comparison shopping or much thought to determine if it is a wise purchase.

COMPARISON SHOP: Know the prices of items that you purchase regularly. Then you can stock up if you spot a good sale. Compare prices of different brands and of the same brand among different stores. Read newspaper ads to compare sale prices. Comparing prices can save you a lot of money, especially on high-priced purchases.

EXAMINE MERCHANDISE: Check items carefully before you buy them. Check for style, quality, color, size, and condition. It is not a good buy if it is out of style, the wrong size, of poor quality, or damaged! If the item is defective, you may be able to return it to the store for an exchange or refund.

ANALYZE ADVERTISING: You are bombarded by television, radio, magazine, newspaper, and in-store advertising trying to sell you products. You must be able to separate the fact from the fiction. Is it really a good sale price? Does that toothpaste make your teeth whiter? Is the item on sale the same one pictured in the ad or a cheaper version? Most stores are honest, but some are not. Advertisements try to play on our emotions and fool us into thinking we cannot live without this item. Do not purchase the item unless you know it is a quality product at a reasonable price!

READ LABELS: Labels contain important information. Read labels to learn the following information before you purchase them.

Clothing labels: **brand name** - who makes it
                    size
                    fiber content - what fibers were used
                    care instructions - how to clean the item

Food Labels: **brand name** - who makes it
                    product description - what is it
                    name and address of the manufacturer
                    net weight
                    ingredients listed in order of quantity present, starting with the
                            largest
                    cooking or storage instructions (optional)
                    nutrition information - serving size
                                    servings per container
                                    calories per serving
                                    nutrient content - fat, cholesterol, sodium, total
                                            carbohydrates, protein, vitamin A, B, C, etc.

These tips can save you money by helping you to avoid unnecessary purchases and make wise shopping decisions.

Additional Activities:

1. Take a field trip to various types of stores to check pricing and services available. Discuss findings.

2. Discuss the best time of year to purchase various items.

3. Use catalogs to compare prices on various items.

4. Compare your local newspaper's grocery store advertisements to the prices of various foods.

5. Ask students to collect five advertisements from magazines. Discuss each ad with the class. Are all of the claims true?

6. Ask each student to bring two labels to class. Discuss the contents of each label with the class.

7. Describe a purchase you made recently that was not a wise purchase. Why?

Name: _____ Date: _____

For the Student

Comparison Shopping Activity

Comparison shopping is comparing prices of the same or similar items at various stores before you make a purchase. This might save you a lot of money on an expensive item.

Visit stores or use catalogs to compare prices of three items. Select one food item, one clothing item, and one electronic item to compare. Get three different prices for each item. Share your findings with the class.

FOOD SHOPPING COMPARISON (examples: potato chips, frozen pizza, etc.)

	Store	Item Description	Cost
1.	_____	_____	_____
2.	_____	_____	_____
3.	_____	_____	_____

CLOTHING SHOPPING COMPARISON (examples: jeans, gym shoes, etc.)

	Store	Item Description	Cost
1.	_____	_____	_____
2.	_____	_____	_____
3.	_____	_____	_____

ELECTRONIC ITEM SHOPPING COMPARISON (examples: CD player, TV., etc.)

	Store	Item Description	Cost
1.	_____	_____	_____
2.	_____	_____	_____
3.	_____	_____	_____

Circle the one you think is the best buy in each comparison.

Name: _____ Date: _____

For the Student

Advertising Activity

Use the sample newspaper sale advertisement on the next page to figure out how much money you can save on your food bill by purchasing items that are on sale. You will need to use your math skills to figure the cost of multiple items and the difference between the regular and sale prices.

ITEM	REGULAR PRICE	SALE PRICE	MONEY SAVED
1. 2 heads lettuce	$0.99 x 2 = $1.98	$0.76 x 2 = $1.52	$1.98 - $1.52 = $0.46
2. 1 box spaghetti	_____	_____	_____
3. 2 lbs. pork chops	_____	_____	_____
4. 3 cans biscuits	_____	_____	_____
5. 2 spaghetti sauce	_____	_____	_____
6. 1 gallon milk	_____	_____	_____
7. 2 lbs. hamburger	_____	_____	_____
8. 2 cake mixes	_____	_____	_____
9. 2 frostings	_____	_____	_____
10. 2 dozen eggs	_____	_____	_____
11. 3 frozen pizzas	_____	_____	_____
12. 2 boxes mac & cheese	_____	_____	_____
13. 1 pkg. hamburger buns	_____	_____	_____
14. 3 boxes gelatin	_____	_____	_____
15. 1 case soda	_____	_____	_____

Total Saved: _____

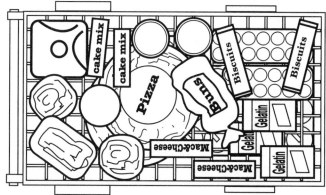

Name: _____ Date: _____

Save-You-More
Market
SUPER SALE THIS WEEK

Gallon 2% Milk reg. $2.19 now **$1.79**	Spaghetti was .99 now **.75**	Hamburger Buns was $1.00 now 2/ **$1.00**
Large Eggs reg. .98 dozen now **.76** dozen	12 oz. Gelatin Mix reg. .33 now **.25**	Wheat Bread reg. $1.49 now only **.99**
Refrigerator Biscuits reg. .30 now 4 for **$1.00**	Cake Mix was $1.09 now **.89**	80% Lean Hamburger was $1.69 lb. now **.99** lb.
24 Can case Soda was $6.39 now **$4.99**	Ready-to-Sread Frosting was $1.29 now **.99**	Center Cut Pork Chops was $2.99 lb now **$1.69** lb
Macaroni and Cheese reg. .48 now 3 for **$1.00**	Half-gallon all flavors Ice Cream was $2.59 now **$1.69**	Head Lettuce was .99 now **.76**
32 oz. Jar Spaghetti Sauce reg. $1.98 On sale for **$1.50**	12" Frozen Pizza was 2.59 now **$1.69**	2 lb Fresh Carrots reg. .79 now **.50**

Name: _____ Date: _____

For the Student: Reading Labels

1. What size is this item? _____

2. What fabric is this made from? _____

_____

3. How should you care for this item? _____

_____

4. What is the brand name? _____

That Girl

Size   12

65% polyester
35% cotton

Machine wash warm.
Tumble dry low.
May need ironing.

5. The brand name is _____

6. The product name is _____

7. The net weight is _____

8. The ingredients are _____

9. The serving size is _____

10. There are _____ servings per container.

11. There are _____ calories per serving.

12. Total fat grams _____   % of daily value _____

13. Cholesterol grams _____   % of daily value _____

14. Sodium grams _____   % of daily value _____

15. Total carbohydrates _____   % of daily value _____

16. Protein _____   % of daily value _____

17. Vitamin A _____   % of daily value _____

18. Dietary Fiber _____   % of daily value _____

19. Iron _____   % of daily value _____

20. Vitamin C _____   % of daily value _____

Nutrition and Fitness

The Food Guide Pyramid

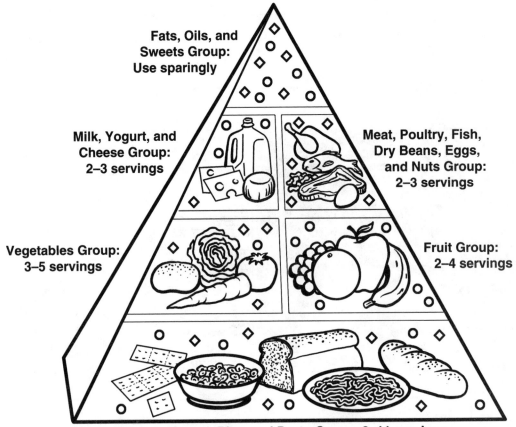

Fats, Oils, and Sweets Group: Use sparingly

Milk, Yogurt, and Cheese Group: 2–3 servings

Meat, Poultry, Fish, Dry Beans, Eggs, and Nuts Group: 2–3 servings

Vegetables Group: 3–5 servings

Fruit Group: 2–4 servings

Breads, Cereal, Rice, and Pasta Group: 6–11 servings

The United States Department of Agriculture developed the Food Guide Pyramid as a healthy guide to eating. It tells us how many of each food group we should eat each day to get the nutrients our body needs to stay fit and healthy. Let's look at each group in the food pyramid.

THE BREADS, CEREAL, RICE, AND PASTA GROUP: This is the largest group that forms the base of the Food Guide Pyramid. You should eat six to 11 servings each day from this group. This group provides carbohydrates, protein, fiber, vitamins, and minerals. Some foods in this group are bread, rolls, bagels, spaghetti, noodles, rice, and cereals. A serving size is one slice of bread, one ounce of cereal, and $\frac{1}{2}$ cup of pasta or rice.

THE VEGETABLE GROUP: This group includes all vegetables. Eat three to five servings from this group each day. Vegetables provide vitamins, minerals, and fiber to our bodies. They are low in fat and calories and high in nutrients. A serving size is $\frac{1}{2}$ cup cooked or raw vegetables, one cup of leafy vegetables, or $\frac{3}{4}$ cup of vegetable juice.

THE FRUIT GROUP: This group includes all fruits. You should eat two to four fruits each day. The fruit can be raw, canned, cooked, dried, or juice. Fruits give us fiber, vitamins, and minerals. A serving size is one medium fruit; $\frac{1}{2}$ cup chopped, cooked, or canned fruit; $\frac{3}{4}$ cup fruit juice; or $\frac{1}{4}$ cup dried fruit.

THE MILK, YOGURT, AND CHEESE GROUP: Eat two to three servings from this group each day. This group includes milk and all foods made from milk such as cheese, ice cream, sour cream, and yogurt. This group provides us with calcium and protein. However, this group is also high in fat. A serving size is one cup of milk or yogurt, $1\frac{1}{2}$ to two ounces of cheese, and $\frac{1}{2}$ cup of ice cream or cottage cheese.

THE MEAT, POULTRY, FISH, DRY BEANS, EGGS, AND NUTS GROUP: You should eat two to three servings from this group each day. These foods are high in protein, B vitamins, zinc, and iron. This group includes meats, eggs, dry beans, peanut butter, and tofu. A serving is three ounces of lean meat, which is the size of a deck of cards, one egg, $\frac{1}{2}$ cup cooked dried beans, four ounces of tofu, $\frac{1}{3}$ cup of nuts, and two tablespoons peanut butter.

THE FATS, OILS, AND SWEETS GROUP: This group forms the small tip of the pyramid, indicating that we should eat only small amounts of these foods. This group includes foods that contain a lot of fat or sugar, such as potato chips, fried foods, candy, soda, and desserts. The fat and sweet symbols are present in all of the food groups to remind us that many foods in the other groups contain fats and sugars. These foods add fat and calories to our diet, but are low in nutrients.

Some foods are called **combination foods** because they are made from foods in more than one food group. You can count them as a serving in more than one food group if they meet the serving size requirement for that group. Some examples of combination foods are pizza, macaroni and cheese, and spaghetti with meat sauce.

If we follow the Food Guide Pyramid we will have a better chance of being healthy and fit.

Additional Activities:

1. Keep a record of all the foods you eat for two or three days. Count the number of foods you eat from each food group each day. Did you meet the pyramid requirements for each group? How can you improve your eating habits?

2. Collect pictures of a variety of foods and form collages of each food group to display in the classroom.

3. Brainstorm to create a list of combination foods on the blackboard. Discuss which food groups each food fits in.

4. Collect pictures of a variety of foods. Draw a food pyramid on the blackboard. Take each picture to the board and place it in the correct food group.

5. List foods that belong in the Fats, Oils, and Sweets Group. Name some healthier foods that we could eat that are low in fats, oils, and sweets.

6. Play a game by going around the room and listing a food in the Vegetable group that begins with the letter "a," then continue around the room naming a food in the group that begins with each letter of the alphabet. Repeat the game with the other food groups.

Name: _____ Date: _____

For the Student

List each food under the correct food group of the Food Guide Pyramid.

butter	cream	ice cream
apple	coffee cake	crackers
macaroni	milk shake	carrots
American cheese	pears	skim milk
hamburger bun	chicken	muffins
french fries	chocolate milk	cranberry juice
turkey	tossed salad	tuna
yogurt	eggs	pudding
asparagus	cottage cheese	orange juice
corn flakes	peach	potatoes
peanut butter	oatmeal	biscuits
rice	liver	peas
applesauce	corn	hamburger
pork chop	cherry pie	raisins
bananas	beef steak	cashews
cauliflower	watermelon	vegetable soup
pancakes	broccoli	

MILK GROUP	VEGETABLE GROUP	MEAT GROUP	FRUIT GROUP	BREAD GROUP
1.	1.	1.	1.	1.
2.	2.	2.	2.	2.
3.	3.	3.	3.	3.
4.	4.	4.	4.	4.
5.	5.	5.	5.	5.
6.	6.	6.	6.	6.
7.	7.	7.	7.	7.
8.	8.	8.	8.	8.
9.	9.	9.	9.	9.
10.	10.	10.	10.	10.

USDA Dietary Guidelines

The United States Department of Agriculture developed the Dietary Guidelines in 1995 to help us choose diets that will meet nutrient requirements, promote health, support active lives, and reduce chronic disease risks. The guidelines apply to children age two and over and all healthy adults. The guidelines are listed below.

1. **EAT A VARIETY OF FOODS.** Use the food guide pyramid to help you select a variety of foods from the various food groups. We need variety to ensure that our bodies get the nutrients they require.

2. **BALANCE THE FOOD YOU EAT WITH PHYSICAL ACTIVITY.** Maintain or improve your weight. Establish healthy eating habits, and exercise to become fit. If you are overweight, try to lose some weight to become healthier.

3. **CHOOSE A DIET WITH PLENTY OF GRAIN PRODUCTS, VEGETABLES, AND FRUITS.** These groups are low in fat and high in vitamins, minerals, carbohydrates, and fiber.

4. **CHOOSE A DIET LOW IN FAT, SATURATED FAT, AND CHOLESTEROL.** This will reduce your risk for heart disease and certain types of cancer. A diet lower in fat will help you maintain a desirable weight.

5. **CHOOSE A DIET MODERATE IN SUGARS.** Foods that are high in sugar usually have lots of calories, but few nutrients. Too much sugar can lead to obesity and tooth decay.

6. **CHOOSE A DIET MODERATE IN SALT AND SODIUM.** Using less salt will reduce the risk of high blood pressure.

7. **IF YOU DRINK ALCOHOLIC BEVERAGES (AS AN ADULT), DO SO IN MODERATION.** Children and young adults should not drink alcoholic beverages. Alcoholic beverages supply calories, but few or no nutrients. Drinking alcohol is also the cause of many health problems and accidents. It can lead to alcoholism.

Additional Activities:

1. Brainstorm to list healthy ways to achieve and maintain a desirable weight.

2. Visit a grocery store and list foods that are advertised as being low fat, fat free, sugar free, and low in sodium. Compare your list with those of your classmates.

3. Write a report about how to prevent high blood pressure, alcoholism, obesity, or heart disease. Share your findings with the class.

Name: _____ Date: _____

For the Student

List ways to follow each of the dietary guidelines listed below.

1. Eat a variety of foods.

_____

_____

_____

2. Balance the food you eat with physical activity.

_____

_____

_____

3. Choose a diet with plenty of grain products, vegetables, and fruits.

_____

_____

_____

4. Choose a diet low in fat, saturated fat, and cholesterol.

_____

_____

_____

5. Choose a diet moderate in sugars.

_____

_____

_____

6. Choose a diet moderate in salt and sodium.

_____

_____

_____

7. If you drink alcoholic beverages (as an adult), do so in moderation.

_____

_____

_____

Nutrients

We follow the Food Guide Pyramid to get all the nutrients our bodies need to be healthy. **Nutrients** are the chemicals found in food that your body needs to keep you healthy and fit. We can get the nutrients our bodies need by eating a variety of foods. The easiest way to eat the right foods is to follow the Food Guide Pyramid. Following is a list of the main nutrients, their functions, and sources.

Nutrient	**Function**	**Food Sources**
Carbohydrates	Main source of energy. Provide fiber for good digestion.	sugars and starches: fruits, vegetables, grains, pasta, honey, sugar
Fats	Give us energy. Add flavor to food. Supply fatty acids the body needs. Carry fat-soluble vitamins. Protect organs and keep us warm.	butter, margarine, meat, nuts, cheese, ice cream, milk
Proteins	Build and repair body cells. Help body systems work properly. Help supply energy.	meats, eggs, fish, poultry, milk, dairy products, dried beans, nuts, peanut butter
Vitamins: Vitamin A	Develops healthy skin. Prevents night-blindness. Helps resist infection.	liver, deep yellow fruits and vegetables, dark green vegetables, milk, egg yolk
B Vitamins riboflavin thiamin niacin	Develops healthy skin, good appetite and diges-tion, and a healthy nervous system.	liver, meat, poultry, eggs, whole grains, milk, dark green leafy vegetables
Vitamin C	Develops strong bones, teeth, and gums. Prevents infection. Helps heal wounds.	citrus fruits, strawberries, cantaloupe, broccoli, cab-bage, potatoes
Vitamin D	Develops strong bones and teeth.	fish oil, fortified milk, sun-light

Nutrient	Function	Food Sources
Minerals: Calcium	Develops strong bones and teeth. Helps blood to clot. Helps heart, nerves, and muscles work properly.	milk, dairy products, green leafy vegetables, canned sardines
Iron	Helps make hemoglobin so the blood can carry oxygen to cells. Helps cells use oxygen.	liver, meat, egg yolk, dried fruit, beans, dark green leafy vegetables, enriched breads and cereals
Sodium	Maintains water balance in the body.	salt

Other minerals eaten in small amounts are iodine, potassium, zinc, copper, magnesium, and phosphorus.

Some health problems can result from too much or too little of specific nutrients. These health problems include:

Health Problem	Cause
overweight or obesity	too much fat in the diet
weak bones and teeth	lack of calcium
high blood pressure	too much sodium
anemia	lack of iron

Additional Activities:

1. List all of the nutrients, functions, and food sources on separate index cards. Mix up the cards and try to match each of the nutrients with its correct functions and food sources.

2. Bring five food labels from home. Check the nutrition information label to see what nutrients are in each food. Discuss good sources of the various nutrients with your class.

3. Collect pictures of food sources for each of the nutrients. Make a collage for each nutrient to display in your class.

Name: _____ Date: _____

For the Student

1. Nutrients are _____
_____

2. We can get the nutrients our body needs by _____
_____

3. Carbohydrates are our main source of _____ . They provide _____ for
   good _____ . The two main forms of carbohydrates are _____ and
   _____ . Sources of carbohydrates are _____ , _____ , and
   _____ .

4. Fats give us _____ . They also add _____ to food. Sources of fat are
   _____ , _____ , and _____ . Too much fat can lead to being
   _____ .

5. Proteins _____ and _____ body cells. They also help the body
   _____ work properly and supply us with _____ . Proteins are found in
   _____ , _____ , and _____ .

6. Vitamin A keeps your _____ healthy. It also helps prevent _____
   _____ and helps your body _____ infection. It is found in _____
   and _____ .

7. The three B vitamins are _____ , _____ , and _____ . They
   help you have healthy _____ and _____ _____ . Foods to eat
   are _____ , _____ , and _____ .

8. Vitamin C helps you have strong _____ , _____ , and _____ .
   It prevents _____ and helps _____ heal. Eat plenty of _____ ,
   _____ , and _____ to get enough vitamin C.

9. Vitamin D gives you strong _____ and _____ . You get your requirements from eating _____ and _____ , and being out in the
   _____ .

10. Calcium makes our _____ and _____ strong. It also helps blood to
    _____ . It helps the _____ , _____ , and _____ work
    properly. Eat plenty of _____ , _____ , and _____ .

11. Iron helps _____ to use _____ . We get iron from _____ ,
    _____ , and _____ . Lack of iron can cause _____ .

12. Sodium comes from _____ . It maintains a balance of _____ in the
    body. Too much sodium may lead to high _____ _____ .

Meal Planning

Meal planning can be fun, but it also takes time and practice to plan meals that are attractive, delicious, economical, and nutritious. You want your menus to have a variety of foods that you and your family enjoy. Follow these guidelines to help you plan meals:

- Use the Food Guide Pyramid to help you plan nutritious meals.

- Cook a variety of foods. Try new recipes so your meals will be exciting!

- Serve meals that contain foods that are different colors, flavors, shapes, textures, and temperatures.

- Read the newspaper grocery sale advertisements before you plan your menus for the week. Include some foods that are on sale to save money.

- Use convenience foods when you are in a hurry. There is a wide variety of frozen foods, canned foods, and boxed mixes that taste great and take little time to prepare.

- Use leftover meats and vegetables to make soups and casseroles.

- Make desserts and casseroles ahead of time and freeze them to use at a later date.

- Use fruits and vegetables when they are in season to save money.

Additional Activities:

1. Look through cookbooks and magazines to find three recipes of foods you would like your family to try. Share these recipes and tell your class why they appeal to you. Ask your parents if you can help prepare these foods for your family meal.

2. Have a tasting party. Bring in a variety of foods. Have the students taste each food and state its flavor and texture.

3. Collect calorie and fat values of foods served at various fast food restaurants. Discuss nutrition problems that are caused by eating at fast food restaurants too often. Brainstorm to come up with healthy food selections at fast food restaurants.

4. Bring a current grocery store advertisement to school. Plan a menu for one full day of meals using only foods that are on sale in the ad.

5. Discuss the advantages and disadvantages of convenience foods. Which convenience foods do you and your family enjoy?

Name: _____ Date: _____

For the Student

Try to create a perfectly nutritious menu for one day. Count to make sure it contains the following Food Guide Pyramid daily requirements:

Milk, Yogurt, and Cheese Group (2–3 servings)
Meat, Poultry, Fish, Dry Beans, Eggs, and Nuts Group (2–3 servings)
Vegetable Group (3–5 servings)
Fruit Group (2–4 servings)
Bread, Cereal, Rice, and Pasta Group (6–11 servings)

BREAKFAST: _____

_____

_____

_____

_____

LUNCH: _____

_____

_____

_____

_____

SUPPER: _____

_____

_____

_____

_____

_____

_____

SNACKS: _____

_____

_____

_____

_____

Name: _____ Date: _____

For the Student: Meal Appeal

We want our meals to be exciting—not boring. We can plan exciting meals by selecting foods that are different colors, flavors, shapes, textures, and temperatures. Complete the following activities to create exciting and nutritious meals!

COLOR: Using foods that are a variety of colors will make your plate of food look more appealing. On your own paper, plan a breakfast menu using foods that are different colors.

FLAVOR: Foods have many different flavors. List three foods that have the following flavors.

Spicy: _____

Sweet: _____

Sour: _____

Bland: _____

SHAPES: Using foods that are different shapes and sizes can make your meal look more appealing. You can change the shape of food by cutting it. Plan a lunch menu including foods that are different shapes. List the food and its shape.

1. _____
2. _____
3. _____
4. _____
5. _____

TEXTURE: Selecting foods with a variety of textures can make your meal more exciting. List three foods that have the following textures.

Crunchy: _____

Sticky: _____

Soft: _____

Chewy: _____

TEMPERATURE: Serve meals including some warm foods and some cold foods for variety. Plan a dinner menu with a combination of warm and cold foods.

1. _____
2. _____
3. _____
4. _____
5. _____

Name: _____ Date: _____

For the Student: Healthy Snacking

We all like to snack between meals and before bedtime. Avoid snacks that have empty calories. **Empty calories** are foods that are high in calories, but have few nutrients. They include foods that have a lot of fats and sugars. Select snacks that will help you meet your Food Guide Pyramid requirements.

List four healthy snacks from each of the four food groups:

MILK, YOGURT, AND CHEESE GROUP:

1. _____
2. _____
3. _____
4. _____

MEAT, POULTRY, FISH, DRY BEANS, EGGS, AND NUTS GROUP:

1. _____
2. _____
3. _____
4. _____

VEGETABLE GROUP:

1. _____
2. _____
3. _____
4. _____

FRUIT GROUP:

1. _____
2. _____
3. _____
4. _____

BREAD, CEREAL, RICE, AND PASTA GROUP:

1. _____
2. _____
3. _____
4. _____

Calories

A **calorie** is a scientific unit of measure that indicates how much energy is released from the burning of food in the body. Your body needs enough food to provide a certain number of calories each day to give you energy and keep your body warm. If the foods you eat contain more calories than your body will burn for energy and heat, your body will take the extra calories and change them to fat. It then stores the fat and you gain weight. If you eat fewer calories than your body needs, your body burns up the fat that is stored and you lose weight. Your body is burning calories even when you are sleeping. The harder you work or exercise, the more calories your body burns.

The number of calories your body needs depends on your age, sex, body size, and activity level. Your activity level is the amount of exercise you get each day. For example: a 15-year-old male needs more calories than a 30-year-old male because of calories needed for growth and additional physical activity.

The National Research Council suggests the following recommended dietary allowances for people of average weight with light to moderate activity levels to maintain their present weight:

Males		Females	
Age	Calories per Day	Age	Calories per Day
11-14	2,500	11-14	2,200
15-18	3,000	15-18	2,200
19-50	2,900	19-50	2,200
51+	2,300	51+	1,900

Those people who engage in hard physical labor or activity for at least four hours per week can add up to 20 percent more calories per day to these figures. People who want to lose weight or who do little physical activity should eat less calories. We should get 30 percent or less of our calories from fats. We can find out how many calories are in the foods we eat from calorie guide books and food labels.

Additional Activities:

1. Check the calories per serving on ten items that you have in your kitchen. Share your findings with the class. Which of the foods have the highest number of calories per serving? Which foods have the lowest number of calories?

2. Keep track of all the foods you eat for one day. Use a calorie guide to total your calories for one day. Did you eat the right amount? How can you improve your calorie intake?

3. Brainstorm a list of foods that are low in calories.

4. Write a short report on one of the following health problems related to eating: bulimia, anorexia, or obesity. Share your report with the class.

Name: _____ Date: _____

For the Student

1. A calorie is

_____

_____

2. Your body uses calories for

_____

_____

3. How can calories affect your weight?

_____

_____

4. List the four factors that determine how many calories you need each day to maintain your current weight.

a. _____

b. _____

c. _____

d. _____

5. What is your recommended calorie allowance per day? _____

What is your dad's recommended calorie allowance per day? _____

Why is there a difference between these allowances?

_____

_____

6. Should people who are overweight eat the recommended allowance for calories if they want to lose weight?

_____

7. How many calories should you eat each day if you practice basketball for 12 hours per week with your team and participate in gym class every day? _____

8. What percent of your calories should come from fats? _____

9. List two ways we can find out the calorie content of foods.

_____

_____

10. List 10 foods that are low in calories.

a. _____ b. _____ c. _____

d. _____ e. _____ f. _____

g. _____ h. _____ i. _____

j. _____

Exercise

Exercise benefits your body in many ways. You just learned that exercise burns calories. If you need to lose a few pounds, you do not have to go on a starvation diet. Just exercise a little more each day to tone your body in a safe and sensible way. If you exercise vigorously or play school sports, your body needs more calories and nutrients to provide the energy required for you to do your best. Balance is the key! You need to balance your physical activity with the number of calories you eat to stay fit and healthy.

Exercise benefits your body in the following ways:

- Exercise strengthens the muscles. It helps your muscles become stronger and more flexible. This gives you better coordination and muscle tone.
- Exercise makes your heart and lungs stronger. This builds your endurance, making it easier for you to exercise for longer periods of time without becoming tired.
- Exercise can reduce the risks of certain diseases. It decreases the risk of heart disease, high cholesterol, high blood pressure, and some forms of cancer.
- Exercise can improve your appearance. It improves blood circulation to give your skin a healthier appearance.
- Exercise can help you relax. It helps your body release stress and tension. This helps you feel more relaxed. It can also help you sleep better.
- Exercise can help you control your weight. It burns calories to keep your body fit and trim. It can help you reach and maintain a healthy weight.
- Exercise can develop self-esteem. If you exercise regularly, you will look good and feel good about yourself.

These are all great reasons to make you want to exercise regularly, but sometimes it is hard to fit exercise into a busy schedule. The Center for Disease Control recommends at least 30 minutes of moderate to intense physical activity every day. Maybe you have the time to schedule specific times each day to jog, do aerobics, or play a sport. If you do, that's great! If you do not have time for planned exercise, just work it into your present activities by taking the stairs instead of the elevator. You could try walking to work or school instead of driving.  There are lots of ways to fit exercise into your day. Be creative, like parking farther from the door so you have to walk farther. Before you realize it, you will look and feel better and exercise will be a regular part of your daily schedule. If you develop a habit of regular exercise now, it will be easier to continue to exercise as you grow older.

Almost every activity you do is a form of exercise. Some activities are more strenuous than others, meaning they burn more calories and provide more benefits for your body. The activity chart on the following page lists some activities you perform and the approximate number of calories that each burns per hour. Learn which activities burn the most calories, and try to fit some of them into your exercise plan.

Activity Chart

Activity	Calories Per Hour
Simple Activities: reading, computing, sewing, playing board games, watching television, sleeping	80-100
Light Activities: office work, school work, walking slowly, cooking	100-160
Moderate Activities: walking moderately fast, light house-work, light gardening	160-240
Intense Activities: heavy housework, bowling, golfing, jogging, skipping rope, hiking, dancing	240-350
Very Intense Activities: swimming, racquetball, basket-ball, running, tennis, bicycling, skiing, football, volleyball, soccer, skating	350-500

Make the effort to fit a variety of exercise activities into your daily routine to help you look and feel much better!

Additional Activities:

1. Keep a fitness diary. Write down all of your exercise for one week. Evaluate your exercise pattern. Do you need to change it? Why?

2. Plan a new fitness activity for your class to participate in with you.

3. Draw posters showing various forms of exercise and the calories burned by each. Display them in the class.

4. Look up the number of calories that you are allowed per day to maintain your present weight. Use the chart above to plan enough exercise to burn up all of those calories. List the exercises and amount of time for each exercise.

5. Invite an aerobics instructor to your class to teach you some aerobics.

6. Brainstorm creative ways to fit exercise into your daily schedule.

Name: _____ Date: _____

For the Student

1. If you eat a snack of two slices of pizza and a soda totaling 600 calories, how long would you need to do the following activities to burn up the calories? Use the activity chart to complete the exercise.

Activity	Calories Burned (per hour)	Hours of Exercise (Round to nearest hour)
example:		
reading	80–100	6 hours
a. walking moderately fast	_____	_____
b. watching television	_____	_____
c. jogging	_____	_____
d. playing soccer	_____	_____
e. school work	_____	_____

2. List eight ways that exercise benefits your body.

   a. _____

   b. _____

   c. _____

   d. _____

   e. _____

   f. _____

   g. _____

   h. _____

3. Develop a fitness plan for a week. Plan at least 30 minutes of physical activity for each day. Include a variety of physical activity.

   Monday: _____

   Tuesday: _____

   Wednesday: _____

   Thursday: _____

   Friday: _____

   Saturday: _____

   Sunday: _____

4. List two creative ways that you can fit exercise into your daily routine if you do not have time for planned exercise.

_____

_____

Drugs and Alcohol

Most teenagers will be faced with the opportunity to use drugs and alcohol. You must be prepared to say "no" to using them. Hopefully knowing the health risks and legal penalties involved with the use of drugs and alcohol will discourage your use of them. The use of most drugs and alcohol by teens is illegal. Drug and alcohol use is also addicting. **Addiction** occurs when the body becomes dependent on the substance and craves its continued use. The body then becomes used to it, and requires more and more to get its effects. It is very hard to stop using drugs and alcohol when you become addicted to them.

Why do teens use tobacco, alcohol, and drugs? Most kids begin using these substances because of pressure from their friends. They think it is cool to smoke, get drunk, or get high. Some kids use illegal substances to escape stress and problems. Some use alcohol and drugs because they are imitating the behavior they see in their adult role models. They are trying to act grown-up by imitating their parents' bad habits. In reality, the use of these substances can make your stress and problems much greater. Kids also use drugs and alcohol to get a high feeling. Many teens do not realize that a short high can cost them their health or their lives.

The following information will teach you the risks involved with using various drugs and alcohol and encourage you to say "no" to their use.

Tobacco: Tobacco contains the drug nicotine. **Nicotine** is a colorless and odorless drug that gives the body a lift when used. It can be smoked in cigarettes and cigars or chewed in snuff or chewing tobacco. Both methods of tobacco use are harmful and addicting. Tobacco use has been linked to causing many types of cancer. It also contributes to heart and lung diseases. Its use by pregnant women can cause babies to have low birth weights, which can in turn cause additional health problems. It also discolors the teeth and causes bad breath. The use of tobacco by teens is illegal in most states.

Many businesses have banned smoking or created specific smoking areas to eliminate passive smoke. **Passive smoke** is the smoke that non-smokers are forced to breathe when others around them smoke. Passive smoke can cause harmful effects on non-smokers.

Harmful effects of smoking can be reversed if a person quits smoking. Studies show that stopping smoking is one of the best steps a smoker can take to improve his or her health. It will improve the breathing lung capacity in a short time. Smoking cessation classes, special gum, and nicotine patches are available to help people stop smoking.

Alcohol: Alcohol is also considered a drug. It is a depressant. A **depressant** slows down activity in the brain and body reflexes. This causes slurred speech and lack of muscle control. It can also cause lack of self-control and poor judgment. Some types of alcohol are beer, wine, and hard liquors, such as scotch, rum, vodka, and whiskey. Excessive drinking of alcohol causes damage to the liver, stomach, esophagus, brain, and the heart. Alcohol use by pregnant women can cause many severe birth defects. Drinking a large amount of alcohol at one time can lead to death by alcohol poisoning. Mixing alcohol with other drugs and medicines can also cause death.

Alcohol use is a leading cause of traffic deaths. Drinking and driving do not mix at any age! Never drink and drive. The penalties by law for drinking and driving are very strict and vary from state to state. The use of alcohol is illegal for anyone under the age of 21.

Dependence upon alcohol leads to the addictive disease called **alcoholism**. Alcoholism can destroy relationships, families, and health. Alcoholics can be treated and recover from alcoholism, but it is a difficult disease to cure.

Drugs: The two different types of drugs are legal drugs and illegal drugs. Both types are addictive and harmful if they are abused. **Drug abuse** means the excessive use of a drug for a purpose other than the one for which it was intended. Drug abuse leads to addiction from **physical dependence** and **psychological dependence** upon the drug. Physical dependence means a person's body is addicted to the drug. Psychological dependence means a person craves the drug to provide an escape from reality. It is very hard to cure drug addiction and dependence.

Legal drugs are drugs that can be purchased legally, but that may be abused. They include over-the-counter drugs, prescription medications, and inhalants that are overused or misused to obtain a high. The most commonly abused legal drugs are pain pills, diet pills, and cold medications. The most common forms of inhalants are spray paint, glue, correction fluid, felt tip markers, nail polish remover, gasoline, and other chemicals. The misuse of these items can lead to damage to the brain, nervous system, kidneys, respiratory system, heart, and chromosomes. Some users have died from using these substances to get high.

Illegal drugs are drugs that are sold privately and are illegal. They include marijuana, cocaine, crack, PCP, LSD, and heroin. These drugs are used by smoking, sniffing, or injecting them into the body. All of them cause serious damage to the body, such as lung damage, reduced resistance to infection, memory loss, emotional problems, seizures, and liver damage. The penalties for use of illegal drugs are high and vary from state to state.

All drug and alcohol abuse can also cause problems within the family and other relationships. Some people are unable to hold down jobs due to their addictions. Others steal to obtain money to support these expensive habits. Many traffic accidents are also caused by people under the influence of drugs and alcohol.

When drugs or alcohol are offered to you, have the good sense to say "no." A few hours of being high are not worth ruining your life.

Additional Activities:

1. Discuss reasons why some people use drugs and alcohol.

2. Write a short paper on the effects of tobacco, alcohol, or drugs.

3. Have speakers discuss tobacco, alcohol, and drug use penalties with the class.

4. Collect advertisements for tobacco and alcoholic beverages. Discuss how advertising influences tobacco and alcohol use.

Name: _____ Date: _____

For the Student

1. List three reasons people use tobacco, drugs, and alcohol.

   a. _____

   b. _____

   c. _____

2. Addiction is

   _____

   _____

3. Nicotine is

   _____

   _____

4. List five health problems associated with tobacco use.

   a. _____

   b. _____

   c. _____

   d. _____

   e. _____

5. Describe passive smoke and the efforts to reduce passive smoke.

   _____

   _____

   _____

6. List three aids to help people stop smoking.

   a. _____

   b. _____

   c. _____

7. What is a depressant?

   _____

   _____

8. Alcoholism is

   _____

   _____

9. List four effects that alcohol has on bodily functions.

   a. _____

   b. _____

   c. _____

   d. _____

Name: _____ Date: _____

10. List two health problems associated with alcohol use and abuse.

    a. _____

    b. _____

11. Why do drugs and alcohol cause so many traffic accidents?

_____

_____

_____

_____

12. List the two types of drugs and three examples of each type.

    A. _____

        1. _____

        2. _____

        3. _____

    B. _____

        1. _____

        2. _____

        3. _____

13. List four health problems associated with drug use.

    a. _____

    b. _____

    c. _____

    d. _____

14. Why does the use of drugs and alcohol destroy many relationships?

_____

_____

_____

15. Why should you say "no" to tobacco, alcohol, and drugs?

_____

_____

_____

_____

Food Preparation

Kitchen Measurements

The secret to successful cooking is measuring ingredients correctly. If you measure an ingredient incorrectly, the food will not taste good and you will waste your time and money.

There are different types of measuring utensils. **Dry measuring cups** are used to measure dry ingredients, such as flour, sugars, butter, shortening, and peanut butter. They are usually made of metal or plastic. They normally come in a set of four cups: 1 cup, $\frac{1}{2}$ cup, $\frac{1}{3}$ cup, $\frac{1}{4}$ cup. A **liquid measuring cup** is used to measure any wet ingredients such as water, milk, oil, or juice. It is made from clear plastic or glass. It has a handle and a pouring spout. The liquid measuring cup is marked with the different measurements ranging from $\frac{1}{4}$ cup to 1 cup on one side, and with metric measurements on the other side. **Measuring spoons** are used to measure small amounts of spices and flavorings. They are made from plastic or metal. They are usually held together by a ring. They usually come in the following sizes: 1 tablespoon, 1 teaspoon, $\frac{1}{2}$ teaspoon, and $\frac{1}{4}$ teaspoon.

Ingredients are measured different ways to get exact measurements. Following are ways to measure various ingredients correctly.

Measuring liquids: Use a liquid measuring cup. Fill to the desired measurement. Place the cup on a flat surface and bend down to check the measurement at eye level. Add a little more or take a little away, until the measurement is exact.

Measuring brown sugar: Use a dry measuring cup. Brown sugar contains moisture and needs to be packed down into the cup for an accurate measure. Push or pack it down tightly into the measuring cup with a spoon. Level the top off with the flat edge of a knife for an exact measurement.

Measuring butter, margarine, or shortening: Use a dry measuring cup to measure these solid fats. Pack the ingredient into the cup and level with a straight edge to get the correct measurement. You may also use the pre-measured sticks of butter or margarine to save time. Each stick of margarine equals $\frac{1}{2}$ cup. The sticks are marked with measurements ranging from 1 tablespoon to $\frac{1}{2}$ cup.

Measuring white flour: White flour must be sifted before it is measured to add air and remove the lumps. Sift the flour onto a piece of waxed paper. Gently spoon the flour into a dry measuring cup. Level off. Don't sift wheat or rye flour, they contain pieces of wheat and rye that should not be removed by the sifter.

Measuring other dry ingredients: Most other dry ingredients such as cocoa, oats, sugar, and chocolate chips should be measured in a dry measuring cup and leveled off to get exact measurements.

Some recipes use abbreviations for measurements. Following are a few abbreviations that you will need to remember.

teaspoon	t. or tsp.	ounce	oz.
tablespoon	T. or Tbsp.	pint	pt.
cup	c.	quart	qt.
pound	lb.	gallon	gal.

Equivalents are different ways to get the same amount of something. There are several equivalents that are useful in cooking. They are:

3 teaspoons	1 tablespoon
16 tablespoons	1 cup
2 cups	1 pint
2 pints	1 quart
4 quarts	1 gallon
8 ounces	1 cup
16 ounces	1 pint
32 ounces	1 quart
128 ounces	1 gallon

If you measure correctly and follow the recipe directions, the foods you prepare will taste great!

Additional Activities:

1. Set up measuring stations for students to practice measuring correctly. Set up stations to measure water, flour, sugar, brown sugar, and butter.

2. Put each ingredient used in a recipe on a separate index card. Have each student in a group select one card and correctly measure the ingredient. Combine all ingredients in the order found in the recipe and prepare the food. Serve it to the class. Discuss the importance of correct measurement.

3. List each of the equivalents parts above on an index card. For example, 3 teaspoons on one card and 1 tablespoon on another card. Mix all of the cards up. Try to match all of the equivalents correctly.

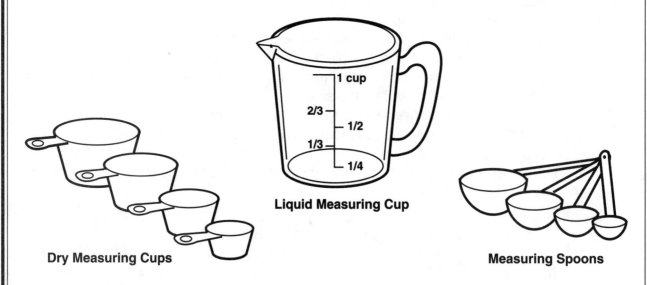

Dry Measuring Cups   **Liquid Measuring Cup**   **Measuring Spoons**

Name: _____ Date: _____

For the Student

1. _____ _____ _____ are used to measure dry ingredients. Some examples of dry ingredients are _____ , _____ , and _____ .

2. A_____ _____ _____ measures liquid ingredients. _____ _____ , and _____ are examples of liquid ingredients. Measure liquids on a _____ _____ at _____ _____ .

3. Measuring spoons measure _____ amounts. They usually come in the following sizes: _____ , _____ , _____ , and _____ . They are made of _____ or _____ and are held together by a _____ .

4. Brown sugar must be _____ into the _____ measuring cup. Then _____ _____ with the flat edge of a knife.

5. _____ , _____ ,and _____ must also be packed into the cup for an _____ measurement.

6. _____ flour must be sifted _____ it is measured. Sift flour onto _____ _____ . Spoon the flour _____ into a _____ _____ _____ . Then _____ off with a _____ . Sifting adds _____ and removes _____ .

7. Write the abbreviations for the following:

   teaspoon   _____   ounce   _____

   tablespoon   _____   pint   _____

   cup   _____   quart   _____

   pound   _____   gallon   _____

8. Write equivalent measurements for the following:

   ___ teaspoons   = 1 tablespoon

   ___ tablespoons   = 1 cup

   ___ cups   = 1 pint

   ___ pints   = 1 quart

   ___ quarts   = 1 gallon

   ___ ounces   = 1 cup

   ___ ounces   = 1 pint

   ___ ounces   = 1 quart

   ___ ounces   = 1 gallon

9. If your measurements are incorrect, the food will taste _____ .

Kitchen Safety

Kitchen safety is very important. The kitchen is not a place to play. More accidents happen in the kitchen than any other room in the house. If you follow these kitchen safety rules, your kitchen will be a safe place.

1. Be sure no one is in your path when you are carrying hot pans of food.
2. Use a thick, dry potholder to pick up hot dishes.
3. When lifting the lid on a hot pan, tip the lid away from you to prevent steam burns.
4. Never leave potholders or things that will burn near the stove burners.
5. Turn off all burners and ovens when you finish using them.
6. Always close cabinet doors and drawers so that you will not bump them.
7. Do not put hot dishes on the counter or table. Place them on a hot pad or trivet.
8. Stir hot foods with a wooden spoon because the handle will stay cool.
9. If you spill something on the floor, wipe it up immediately.
10. Sweep up broken glass immediately. Do not try to pick it up with your hands.
11. Do not place sharp knives in the sink. They could be unnoticed under soapy water.
12. Use a cutting board for chopping and slicing foods.
13. Cut away from your body with a knife.
14. Do not wear loose, baggy clothes around the stove.
15. Never throw water on a grease fire. Use salt or baking soda.
16. Keep all pot handles toward the center of the stove.
17. Do not touch electrical appliances with wet hands.
18. Be very careful when walking with a knife. Point it toward the floor.
19. Never put your hand in the garbage disposal.
20. If a fire starts, leave the house immediately and go to the nearest phone.
21. Let hot pans cool down before you place them in the water.
22. Use sharp knives to cut and slice. A dull knife must be pressed and could slip.

Additional Activities:

1. Make kitchen safety posters to display.

2. Role-play the correct way to follow safety rules.

3. Help the students make pot holders, hot pads (for holding hot dishes), or even a homemade cooling rack for cookies, pies, cakes.

Name: _____ Date: _____

For the Student

Place a T in the blank if the statement is true and an F in the blank if it is false.

_____ 1. Walk with the point of a sharp knife toward the floor.

_____ 2. Cut away from your body with a knife.

_____ 3. Never leave a cookbook near the stove burner.

_____ 4. If you spill something on the floor, leave it for the dog.

_____ 5. Leave cabinet doors and drawers open so you can find things.

_____ 6. Use a towel to pick up hot pans from the stove.

_____ 7. If grease catches on fire, throw lots of water on it.

_____ 8. Chop foods on the counter top.

_____ 9. Turn off all burners and the oven when you finish using them.

_____ 10. Dry your hands before touching an electrical appliance.

_____ 11. Be sure your path is clear before carrying hot pans of food.

_____ 12. Do not place a sharp knife into the soapy water.

_____ 13. Stir hot foods with a metal spoon because the handle will stay cool.

_____ 14. When lifting the lid on a hot pot, tip the lid towards yourself.

_____ 15. Push the food down in the garbage disposal with your hand.

_____ 16. Keep pot handles turned toward the center of the stove.

_____ 17. If you have a fire in the kitchen, leave the house and get help.

_____ 18. Don't wear baggy clothes around the stove.

_____ 19. Use a dull knife to chop and slice food.

_____ 20. Place the hot cookie sheet in the water to soak.

Food Storage and Kitchen Cleanliness

Everything we touch has bacteria on it. Bacteria are found on pets, pests, people, objects, and in the air. Bacteria need food, moisture, and warm temperatures to grow. Some bacteria are helpful and are used to make cheese, yogurt, and medicines. Others are harmful and can cause sickness and food poisoning. Some types of food poisoning are like the flu, but others are deadly. We must practice kitchen cleanliness and store foods properly to cut down on germs and food spoilage. If you do not handle food carefully and keep your kitchen as clean as possible, you could get food poisoning. These tips will help you make and keep your kitchen a safe and healthy place to prepare and serve food.

1. Always wash your hands with warm soapy water for at least 20 seconds before you touch food. Clean under the nails, too. Wash your hands often when working with food.
2. Keep your hands away from your face, hair, and pets while cooking and eating.
3. Do not cough or sneeze on the food or equipment.
4. Use plastic cutting boards rather than wooden ones, because bacteria can live in wood and plastic is easier to clean because bacteria can live in the wood.
5. Keep your cooking area clean.
6. Make sure equipment and utensils are clean before you use them.
7. Wash kitchen towels and cloths often.
8. Store foods in the proper place when you return from grocery shopping.
9. Keep hot foods at or above 140° Fahrenheit, and cold foods below 40° Fahrenheit. The danger zone for food spoilage is between 40° and 140° Fahrenheit. Hot temperatures over 140° kill bacteria and cold temperatures slow down bacteria growth.
10. Thaw foods in the refrigerator, not on the kitchen counter.
11. Some signs of food spoilage are mold, funny smells, color changes, and texture changes. If you think a food might be spoiled, DO NOT EAT IT! THROW IT AWAY!!
12. Marinate foods in the refrigerator, not at room temperature.
13. Cover and refrigerate leftovers immediately after meals. Do not leave them sitting out to cool because harmful bacteria can form in a short time.
14. If you are going on a picnic, keep food in a cooler to prevent spoilage.
15. Do not work with food if you have an open cut or sore on your hands.

Additional Activities:

1. Have each student inspect his or her home kitchen and list any sanitation mistakes. Each student should report the findings to the class and to his or her parents!

2. Make posters showing sanitation tips to display in your classroom.

3. Research a type of food poisoning and write a short report. Share the report with the class.

Name: _____ Date: _____

For the Student

Place a T in the blank if the statement is true. Place an F in the blank if it is false.

_____ 1. Allow pets to lick your plate after you finish eating.

_____ 2. It is all right to prepare food if you have an open cut on your hand.

_____ 3. Wash your hands for at least 20 seconds before touching food.

_____ 4. Clean your cooking area once a week.

_____ 5. Serve the apples as soon as they are picked.

_____ 6. If the food looks or smells spoiled, you should throw it away.

_____ 7. Keep hot foods above 100° Fahrenheit.

_____ 8. You can eat the bread if it has a little mold on it.

_____ 9. Bacteria need food, moisture, and cold temperatures to grow.

_____ 10. Wash your hands after using the restroom.

_____ 11. You may lick the spoon and then stir the food.

_____ 12. Thaw foods on the kitchen counter.

_____ 13. Keep cold foods below 40° Fahrenheit.

_____ 14. Cover and refrigerate leftovers immediately.

_____ 15. Wash your hands with cold water before handling food.

_____ 16. Temperatures over 140° Fahrenheit kill bacteria.

_____ 17. Keep food for a picnic in a cooler.

_____ 18. Cold temperatures slow down the growth of bacteria.

_____ 19. Leave food sitting on the table for a few hours after you eat to allow it to cool off before you refrigerate it.

_____ 20. Some bacteria are helpful.

Name: _____ Date: _____

_____ 21. Some types of food poisoning can kill you.

_____ 22. Bacteria are also called germs.

_____ 23. Leave your milk and eggs in the trunk of the car for several hours before they are put away.

_____ 24. Everything we touch carries bacteria.

_____ 25. Bacteria are used to make some types of medicine.

_____ 26. It is okay to brush your hair while you are cooking.

_____ 27. Wash kitchen towels and cloths once a month.

_____ 28. Marinate food in the refrigerator.

_____ 29. Wash your hands after petting the dog.

_____ 30. Use the kitchen towel to wipe your mouth.

Circle the correct answer.

1. Mary just served a turkey with all of the trimmings to her family for Thanksgiving dinner. She should:

   a. Cover the food and leave it on the counter until supper time.

   b. Place the food in small containers, cover, and refrigerate immediately.

   c. Relax for a few hours before refrigerating the leftovers.

2. Jim went to the grocery store for his mother. He purchased milk, eggs, hamburger, and buns. He should:

   a. Leave the food in the truck while he plays basketball for two hours.

   b. Drop the food off at home and leave it on the table for his mother to put away when she gets home from work in a few hours.

   c. Go home and place the milk, eggs, and hamburger in the refrigerator.

Table Manners

Table manners are very important. Others watch you when you are eating. You want to make a good impression by showing good manners when you eat. **Table manners** or **etiquette** are rules or guidelines for eating politely. Manners may be less formal at home or school than at a fancy restaurant or banquet. Manners may vary in different countries. What is acceptable in the United States may be rude behavior in another country. The manners below are acceptable for the United States.

1. Arrive at the table with clean hands, face, and nails, and dress appropriately.
2. Sit straight in your chair with your feet flat on the floor. Keep your elbows off the table.
3. Keep your hands on your lap when you are not eating.
4. Wait until everyone in the group is eating before you begin to eat.
5. Lay your napkin across your lap. Use it to wipe your lips and mouth when necessary.
6. Cut food into small bites before eating.
7. Finger foods are foods that you may pick up with your fingers to eat. Some examples of finger foods are fried chicken, sandwiches, pizza, pickles, chips, and french fries.
8. Tear or cut bread and rolls in half before you butter and eat them.
9. Never talk with food in you mouth.
10. Eat slowly and chew with your mouth closed.
11. Never comb your hair or apply makeup at the table.
12. Do not reach for food. Politely ask someone to pass it to you.
13. Pass food to the right.
14. Place your used silverware on your plate while you are using it.
15. Turn your head away from the table and cover your mouth if you cough or sneeze.
16. Do not pick up a bowl and drink from it. Use your spoon.
17. If you have several forks and spoons at your place setting, use the ones on the outside first and work toward the center of your plate.
18. When you finish eating, place your napkin next to your plate and place your silverware on your plate.
19. Talk only about pleasant things while you are eating.
20. Ask to be excused before you leave the table.

Additional Activities:

1. Make posters showing table manners and display them.

2. Role-play good table manners.

3. Role-play poor table manners.

Name: _____ Date: _____

For the Student

1. Table manners are _____

_____

2. Why should you use good table manners?_____

_____

Place a T in the blank if the statement is true. Place an F in the blank if it is false.

_____ 3. Your hands, face, and nails should be clean when you come to the dinner table.

_____ 4. It is all right to begin eating before your mother sits down.

_____ 5. You may lean your elbows on the table.

_____ 6. Sit up straight in your chair at the table.

_____ 7. Reach across the table to get the bowl of corn.

_____ 8. Pass food to who wants it directly, no matter where they're sitting.

_____ 9. Place the dirty knife next to your plate.

_____ 10. Place your napkin on your lap.

_____ 11. Keep your hands on your lap while you are not eating.

_____ 12. Tuck your napkin under your chin.

_____ 13. Cut food into small bites before eating.

_____ 14. Pick up a steak to eat it.

_____ 15. Tear the roll in half before you eat it.

_____ 16. Talk with food in your mouth.

_____ 17. Eat slowly and chew with your mouth closed.

_____ 18. Comb your hair at the table if it is messy.

_____ 19. Do not make rude noises at the table.

_____ 20. If you have two forks, use the one next to your plate first.

Table Settings

A complete setting for one person is called a **cover**. This includes:

flatware:	knives, forks, and spoons
glassware:	beverage glasses
dinnerware:	plates, bowls, and cups
linens:	napkins, place mats, and tablecloths

The items included in the cover will vary based upon the following:

meal style:	formal meal, informal meal, or buffet
foods served:	use only the necessary utensils for the foods you are serving

The table may be decorated with a centerpiece, place cards, and party favors, depending on the occasion. If the cover has more than one fork or spoon, begin with the one farthest from the plate for the appetizer. The one closest to the plate is for the main dish or dessert. Remember to work from the outside edges, toward the center of your plate.

Below is a sample cover showing the placement of most possible items. Place each cover one inch from the table edge. Use only the items required for the foods you are serving.

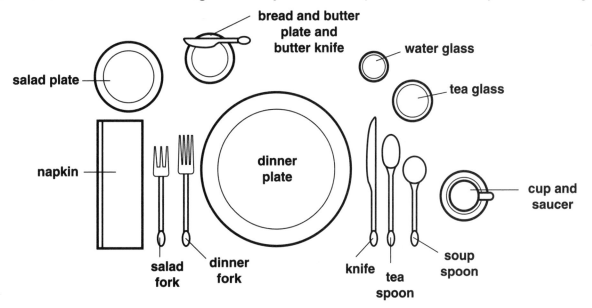

Additional Activities:

1. Give each student a paper place mat. Have them draw a sample cover with correct placement of all flatware, glassware, dinnerware, linens. Practice setting covers.
2. Brainstorm ways to decorate the table for birthdays and holidays.
3. Cut sample table settings from magazines and display them.
4. Have each student write a menu on an index card. Mix the cards and allow each student to pick one card and set the table correctly for that menu.

Name: _____ Date: _____

For the Student: Table Settings

1. What is wrong with this cover?

_____

_____

_____

_____

_____

2. What is wrong with this cover?

_____

_____

_____

_____

_____

3. Draw a cover for the following menu: bacon, eggs, toast, milk, and orange juice.

4. Draw a cover for the following menu: shrimp cocktail, tossed salad, dinner roll, steak, baked potato, iced tea, coffee.

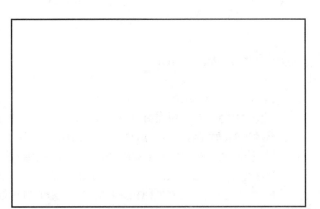

No-Cook Recipes for Classroom Use

The following recipes may be used to prepare foods in a normal classroom. They do not require the use of a stove, but some require small electrical appliances. The teacher will need to provide the proper equipment and ingredients for each cooking experience. Adjust the recipes according to the number of students in each group and enjoy eating.

Milk, Yogurt, and Cheese Group Recipes

Milk Shake   Serves 3

Ingredients:
vanilla ice cream
milk
flavorings:
    3 Tbsp. chocolate syrup, $\frac{1}{2}$ cup strawberries, or 1 banana

Equipment:
blender
measuring cups
ice cream dipper
glasses

Directions:
1. Place 5 scoops ice cream in the blender.
2. Add 1 cup milk. Add flavoring, if desired.
3. Beat for 2 minutes or until thickened.

Easy Cheese Cake   Serves 8-10

Ingredients:
12 oz. whipped topping
8 oz. cream cheese
1 c. powdered sugar
2 graham cracker pie crusts
1 can cherry pie filling

Equipment:
electric mixer
large mixing bowl
measuring cups
spatulas/wooden spoons
plates, forks, knife

Directions:
1. Place whipped topping, cream cheese, and powdered sugar into large mixing bowl. Beat on medium until smooth.
2. Spread evenly into the 2 pie crusts.
3. Spread cherry filling evenly on top of each crust.
4. Refrigerate until firm.
5. Cut and serve.

Vegetable Group Recipes

Garden Salad

Ingredients:
lettuce
tomatoes/cucumber
carrots/celery
broccoli/cauliflower
cheese/bacon bits/croutons
(more toppings if desired)
various salad dressings

Equipment:
bowls
grater
paring knives
cutting boards
bowls, spoons, forks

Directions:
1. Wash and chop all the vegetables. Allow students to help if they are able.
2. Grate cheese (if needed).
3. Place each ingredient in a separate bowl.
4. Let each person create his/her own individual salad and dressing.

Salsa

Ingredients:
2 peeled tomatoes
1-4 oz. rinsed green chiles
1 small chopped onion
1 tsp. olive oil
$\frac{1}{4}$ c. chopped celery
$\frac{1}{4}$ tsp. salt
$\frac{1}{4}$ tsp. pepper

Equipment:
blender
cutting board
paring knife
measuring cups/spoons
bowls, spoons, plates

Directions:
1. Place all ingredients in blender, chop until chunky.
2. Serve with tortilla chips and guacamole.

Guacamole

Ingredients:
2 peeled, seeded avocados
$\frac{1}{2}$ small chopped onion
2 Tbsp. lemon juice
1 clove peeled garlic

Equipment:
blender
paring knife
cutting board
bowl, spoons, plates

Directions:
1. Place all ingredients in blender and blend until smooth.
2. Serve with chips and salsa.

Fruit Group Recipes

Fruit Face Salad

Ingredients:
canned peach halves
canned pear halves
cottage cheese
grated American cheese
raisins
apples
maraschino cherries
lettuce

Equipment:
knives
grater
spoons, plates, bowls

Directions:
1. Place a lettuce leaf on each plate.
2. Place a peach or a pear half on the lettuce with the rounded side up.
3. Add cottage cheese or grated cheese for hair.
4. Decorate with raisins for eyes, cherry for nose, and an apple wedge for the mouth.

Crunchy Banana Boats

Ingredients:
1 medium banana
cream cheese/peanut butter
granola

Equipment:
paring knife
serving spoons
spreading knives
plates, forks, spoon

Directions:
1. Slice a banana in half lengthwise.
2. Spread cut sides with cream cheese or peanut butter.
3. Sprinkle with granola.
4. Top with other banana half.

Breads, Cereal, Rice, and Pasta Group Recipes
Pita Pockets

Ingredients:
pita bread
ranch salad dressing
lettuce
cucumbers
bean sprouts
chopped deli meats
grated cheese

Equipment:
bowls
cutting board
knives
plates, spoons

Directions:
1. Prepare ingredients in separate serving containers.
2. Cut pitas in half and open the pocket.
3. Spread salad dressing inside.
4. Allow students to add desired fixings.

Wonderful Wafflewich

Ingredients:
frozen waffles
peanut butter
sliced bananas

Equipment:
toaster
spreading knives
cutting board
paring knife

Directions:
1. Toast a waffle.
2. Cut it in half diagonally.
3. Spread each half with peanut butter.
4. Top one half with banana slices.
5. Top with other waffle half.

Meat, Poultry, Fish, Dry Beans, Eggs, and Nuts Group Recipes
Meat Kabob

Ingredients:
hot dogs
ham
pineapple chunks
olives
cheese
dill dip

Equipment:
cutting boards
paring knives
skewers
plates, forks

Directions:
1. Cut meat, cheese, and fruits into bite sized chunks.
2. Place all choices in separate containers.
3. Fill a skewer, place some dip on plates for dipping sauce.

Drum Roll

Ingredients:
small flour tortillas
peanut butter
jams and jellies
apples (chopped)
raisins
sunflower seeds

Equipment:
spreading knives
paring knives
cutting board
serving spoons
plates

Directions:
1. Place each ingredient in a separate serving container.
2. Spread a tortilla with peanut butter and jelly.
3. Allow each student to select desired toppings for the tortilla.
4. Roll the tortilla and serve.

Grooming

Your Grooming Routine

Grooming is taking care of yourself and trying to always look your best. Your appearance sends a nonverbal message to everyone who sees you. Your appearance is the first impression people receive about you. You want that to be a positive impression. Cleanliness and neatness are the keys to good grooming. If your body, hair, teeth, hands, and clothing are neat and clean, you will look well-groomed. Developing good grooming habits and a grooming routine will keep you looking your best all of the time.

Body Care: Caring for your body includes bathing, shaving, skin care, and fitness. **Bathing** daily with soap and water will remove perspiration, dirt, oil, and dead skin cells. **Perspiration** is sweat. When perspiration mixes with bacteria on your skin, it forms **body odor**. Body odor can be prevented by using deodorant and antiperspirant under your arms following your bath or shower. **Deodorant** controls the body odor by stopping bacteria growth. **Antiperspirants** reduce perspiration as well as control the body odor. They can be purchased in the form of a spray, roll-on, stick, or powder. Select the deodorant or antiperspirant that is most effective for you. You may need to bathe and apply deodorants or antiperspirants more frequently if you play in sports or are very active.

Many adolescents choose to begin **shaving**. When you begin to shave is a very individual decision. Some people begin unwanted hair growth sooner than others. Boys shave to control unwanted facial hair. Girls shave to control unwanted underarm and leg hair. Do not begin shaving until it is really necessary. For most people, once they begin shaving, they need to continue shaving because the hair that grows back is more coarse than before. Apply soap lather or shaving cream to the area to help the razor glide smoothly and avoid skin irritation. You may apply a moisturizing cream or aftershave product to keep your skin moist after shaving. You may choose to use a disposable razor or an electric razor.

Skin Care: You need to keep your skin looking healthy by keeping your skin clean, getting plenty of exercise and sleep, eating healthy, and protecting your skin from the sun's damaging rays.

Your skin may be normal, oily, dry, or a combination of these skin types. Few people are lucky enough to have normal healthy skin. You should clean and moisturize normal skin regularly to keep it looking healthy.

Many teens have oily skin. Oily skin needs washed often to prevent pimples and acne. **Acne** is a skin disorder that results in the appearance of blemishes on the face, neck, scalp, upper chest, or back. Many products may be purchased to cleanse oily facial skin and control acne. If acne becomes a serous problem for you, seek the help of a **dermatologist**, or skin specialist.

Dry skin results in flakiness and roughness of the skin. If your skin is dry, you need to apply a moisturizer or lotion to the dry areas regularly.

Combination skin types are the most common skin types. If you have combination skin, you probably have an oily area called the T-zone. The **T-zone** is your forehead, nose, and chin. The T-zone area of the face is usually oily while the areas around your eyes and cheeks will be dry. Be sure to remove the oil from the T-zone by cleaning it regularly. Avoid excess scrubbing of the dry areas. Use only moisturizer on the dry areas.

The Sun can cause permanent damage to your skin. If you enjoy being outside in the summer, be sure to apply a sunscreen. **Sunscreen** is a product that filters out some of the Sun's damaging rays. Sunscreens are rated by degree of protection. The higher the SPF number, the greater protection it offers. **SPF** stands for **Sun Protection Factor**. Reapply sunscreen after you wash, swim, or sweat heavily. If you begin protecting your skin when you are young, you may prevent premature wrinkling and skin cancer.

Girls may wish to begin using facial makeup in their early teens. Learn to apply makeup correctly to achieve a natural look. Too much makeup is unflattering. Many department stores offer free lessons in applying makeup properly.

Fitness: Fitness means to keep your body fit by exercising daily and eating a variety of healthy foods. Include a variety of exercises in your weekly exercise routine and follow the Food Guide Pyramid requirements to stay fit and trim.

Dental Care: You want to have healthy teeth and gums for a great smile. If you develop good dental hygiene habits when you are young, your teeth and gums will look and feel great. Brush your teeth with toothpaste after each meal and snack if possible. Brushing removes plaque and tartar. **Plaque** is an invisible film of bacteria that forms on your teeth and causes cavities and gum disease. **Tartar** is plaque that is not removed and becomes hardened. It forms between teeth and in areas that are hard to reach with your toothbrush. It must be removed by your dentist. Flossing daily between the teeth will help reduce the buildup of plaque and tartar. Using mouthwash regularly following brushing to kill bacteria will keep your breath fresh. Visit your dentist regularly to check for cavities and have your teeth professionally cleaned. Most dentists recommend checkups once or twice per year.

Nail Care: Your hands and nails are very visible and should always look neat and clean. A weekly manicure should be part of your regular grooming routine. A **manicure** is treatment and care of your fingernails and hands. Begin a manicure by filing and shaping your nails with an emery board or a nail file. Soak your hands in warm water to soften the cuticles. **Cuticles** are the skin that grows at the base of every nail. Use a nail tool to gently push back the cuticles. Complete the manicure by applying a moisturizing lotion to prevent dryness. Girls may choose to apply nail polish at this time.

A **pedicure** is treatment and care of the toenails and feet. It involves steps similar to a manicure and should be performed every few weeks. Using clippers, you should trim your toenails straight across to prevent ingrown nails. You may smooth the edges with an emery board. Use a pumice stone to remove dead skin from your feet. Apply lotion to keep your feet smooth and soft. Foot sprays or powders may be applied to reduce foot odor.

Hair Care: Many hair care products are available for different hair types, such as oily, dry, limp, damaged, or normal. Ask your hair stylist what type of hair you have if you are not sure. Your hair type will dictate how often you need to wash your hair and which products you should use. Wash it regularly to remove oil, dirt, and dead skin from your hair and scalp. You may choose to apply a conditioner to reduce tangles and give your hair more body.

Have your hair cut or styled regularly to remove split ends and keep you looking your best. Choose a hair cut or style that looks good on you and fits your lifestyle. You will want a style that is easy and convenient for you to care for. Most stylists have many books available to give you an idea for a new cut or style. Ask your stylist for tips to help you style your own hair each day.

Looking your best makes you feel your best and is the key to a healthy, happy you.

Additional Activities:

1. Make a list of all the grooming products you use each day. Discuss the list with the class.

2. Select one grooming product (for example: shampoo). Visit a store and list all of the types and brands of the product available. Discuss your findings with the class. Were you surprised at how many products are available? What are the differences? Is there much difference in the prices?

3. Invite the following guest speakers to your class:
   • dermatologist.
   • hair stylist.
   • barber.
   • makeup demonstrator.
   • dentist.
   • manicurist.

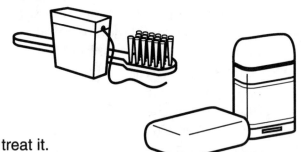

4. Write a short report on acne and how to treat it.

5. Cut out pictures from magazines of people who are well-groomed and people that are poorly groomed. Display them in collages in the classroom.

6. Cut out advertisements for various grooming products. Display them on posters in the classroom.

7. Select one new grooming product that you have never used before. Use it for one week and report on it to your class. Was it a good product? Did it do the job you thought it would do? Will you purchase it again? Would you recommend it to your classmates?

Personal Care Schedule

The following is a guide for a grooming schedule to help each student develop good grooming habits. List each task and determine how often to perform it. Place the schedule in a location that is visible to you and follow it. Follow the example provided and list each grooming task that you perform.

GROOMING TASK	DAILY	WEEKLY	AS NEEDED
brush my hair	several times per day		

Name: _____ Date: _____

For the Student

Fill in the blanks.

1. Grooming means taking _____ of yourself and _____ to look your

   _____.

2. You need to take proper care of your _____ , _____ , _____ ,

   _____ , and _____ in order to be well-groomed.

3. Bathing _____ with _____ and _____ will remove _____.

4. _____ is sweat. When it mixes with bacteria on your skin, it forms

   _____ _____.

5. Body odor can be prevented by using _____ or _____.

6. You may need to shower _____ often if you participate in _____.

7. _____ controls the growth of unwanted hair.

8. Your skin type may be _____ , _____ , _____ , or _____.

9. _____ skin needs to be washed more often than other types.

10. _____ skin needs to have moisturizer applied regularly.

11. See a _____ if you are unable to control your acne.

12. The oily area containing your forehead, nose, and chin is called the _____.

13. Protect your skin from damage by the _____ by using _____.

14. Brush your teeth after each _____ or _____ if possible.

15. Use _____ to clean the _____ between your teeth.

16. Visit your dentist for check-ups _____ or _____ a year.

17. A _____ is the treatment and care of your fingernails and hands. A

    _____ is the treatment and care of your feet and toenails.

18. Wash your hair regularly to remove _____, _____, and _____

    _____.

19. Choose a _____ _____ that looks good on you and fits your _____.

Clothing Selection and Care

You will want to select clothing and shoes that will help you look your best and feel comfortable. Your clothes send a message to the people you meet. Wear clothes that are appropriate and fit the situation. You would select different clothes for a party than you would for a football game. You want to select clothing that will help you feel comfortable in each situation. Become aware of the clothing that is worn in various situations and for different occasions. Be sure to include a variety of clothes in your wardrobe for the various situations and occasions you might come across.

Fit: Select clothes that fit you correctly. Clothing that is too baggy looks sloppy. Clothes that are too tight are uncomfortable and emphasize body imperfections. Select shoes that fit to avoid permanent damage to your feet.

Color: Select colors that match and look good on you. Certain colors will look better with your hair and skin tone. Experiment with different colors by draping fabrics of various colors around your neck to frame your face. Note the colors that look best on you. You may want to attend a color seminar held by a clothing store to obtain professional advice about which clothing and make-up colors look best on you. Lighter colors make objects appear larger, while darker colors make them appear smaller. Keep this in mind to help you camouflage body imperfections. Most people look good in a variety of colors. Create different outfits by mixing clothing items that coordinate in color. Build your wardrobe around the colors that make you look and feel your best.

Design: The design lines of fabrics and garments can make you appear taller, shorter, larger, or smaller. Design lines have direction. They are vertical, horizontal, or diagonal. The eye will follow the direction of the lines. Horizontal lines will make an object appear wider, while vertical lines give an object the effect of height or have a slenderizing effect. Diagonal lines are slenderizing because they draw the eye at an angle across the body. Tucks, pleats, trims, and neckline shapes can produce the same effects. Select jackets and skirts that are a length that is most suitable to your height and shape. Use design lines to emphasize your good points and camouflage your bad ones.

Fabric: Select fabrics that complement your shape and size. Lightweight fabrics that hang in soft folds are flattering to everyone. Clingy fabrics will show any body imperfections. Stiff or bulky fabrics will make an object appear larger. Combine fabrics to achieve the look that is most flattering for you.

Fashion: Fashion is a style accepted by a large number of people at a particular time. Clothing fashions and styles tend to change rapidly. Current fashion and styles vary from one part of the world to the next, or even from city to city. Age, income, lifestyles, and many other factors affect when or how we accept new fashions.

Classics are styles that endure over a long period of time. They include clothes that have simple, uncluttered lines. Some examples of classic clothing are jeans, trousers, cardigan sweaters, tuxedos, shirtwaist dresses, double-breasted jackets, and trench coats. These styles have continued to be popular for a number of years. You should include some of the classic styles in your wardrobe because they will remain in style for a long time.

Fads are fashions that have a short life-span. They are quickly accepted by a small segment of the population, but leave the fashion scene after a short amount of time. Fads are usually readily available, inexpensive, and extreme or exaggerated in design. Shoes and accessories are often subject to fads. Some examples of recent fads are platform shoes, bell bottom pants, mini skirts, halter tops, jam shorts, and big earrings. Many of these fads will die out only to return again in a few years.

The fashion cycle is the repetition of fashions regularly every 17 to 20 years. Each year's fashions are influenced by those that were popular around 20 years ago. The cycle continues to repeat itself. Large clothing manufacturers and retailers employ fashion forecasters to assess trends in the world around them to project fashions for a couple of years in the future. They look at the fashion cycle, lifestyles, technology, current events, art, economics, politics, and international influences to predict the fashions of the near future. Some of the fashions they select become popular, while others are flops or fads. In order for a fashion to become popular, it must be recognized and accepted. The fashion industry uses fashion magazines, newspapers, television, fashion shows, and public celebrities to promote their fashions to the general public. As soon as the public accepts something as a style, the fashion industry will look for a new style or trend to promote. Trying to keep up with fashion trends can be fun and exciting, but very costly.

The following criteria will help you make wise clothing choices that are suitable to your needs. Purchase clothing items that meet the criteria that are important to you.

1. Does the garment reflect your self-image and lifestyle?
2. Does the clothing contribute to your feeling of self-esteem?
3. Will it gain approval from the group that is important to you?
4. Will it make you more effective professionally or socially?
5. Does it enhance your appearance in a positive way?
6. Does it provide an outlet for personal creativity and self-expression?
7. Is it comfortable and functional?
8. Is the cost within your budget?
9. Is the quality and workmanship acceptable?
10. Is it easy to care for?

Additional Activities:

1. Interview friends and family members the appropriate ages concerning fashions 50–70 years ago, 25–35 years ago, and 10–15 years ago. Collect photographs of the fashions from these time periods. Can you see the fashion cycle repeating itself? Give examples.

2. Invite the following guest speakers to the classroom: a color consultant, a fashion designer, a fabric store owner, and a department store buyer.

3. Select an article of clothing that you might like to purchase. See if it meets the criteria for clothing selection. Will you purchase the item? Will it be a wise purchase?

Name: _____   Date: _____

For the Student

1. Write the name of an item of clothing that you feel sends the following messages.

   sloppy _____

   revealing _____

   feminine _____

   masculine _____

   sporty _____

   conservative _____

   wild _____

   neat _____

   tasteless _____

2. List your 10 favorite articles of clothing in your current wardrobe.

   _____

   _____

   _____

   _____

   Why are they your favorites?

   _____

   _____

3. List your five least favorite articles of clothing in your current wardrobe.

   _____

   _____

   Why are they your least favorites?

   _____

   _____

4. List five current fashions that are fads.

   _____

   _____

5. List three people who dress in a manner you admire.

   _____

   Why did you select these people?

   _____

   _____

   Do you dress in a similar style?

   _____

Manners

Manners are guidelines for polite behavior. You have already learned about table manners. Now we will look at manners for daily behavior. Displaying good manners will send a positive message about you to the people you meet. People with good manners make a good impression on others. Some manners guidelines to follow are listed below.

1. Introductions
   a. Introduce others by saying something like this: "Jane, I would like for you to meet my friend Joe." "Joe, this is my sister Jane." The name of the older of the two people being introduced or the female should be spoken first.
   b. Stand when introduced to someone if it is appropriate to do so.
   c. Shake the hand of the person when you are introduced.

2. Telephone manners
   a. Answer the phone politely.
   b. Take a message if someone is not available to come to the phone.
   c. Don't yell in the caller's ear.

3. Remember to use the words "please" and "thank you."

4. Listen attentively to the conversations of others.

5. Do not interrupt when someone is talking.

6. Open the door for your date or an adult in your company.

7. Always wait your turn in line.

8. Always move over to the side of a walk to make room for others to pass by.

9. Do not be loud or obnoxious.

10. Respect the rights of others.

Additional Activities:

1. Practice introductions.

2. Practice telephone manners.

3. Discuss manners that you have observed. Offer alternatives that should have been used.

Careers

Exploring Careers

A **career** is the work a person does and the jobs that a person holds over a number of years. Most people have many different jobs during their lifetimes. The different jobs you have are also called **occupations**. Do you have any ideas about what career you would like in the future?

People work for different reasons. The main reasons that people work are for:

1. Money—to pay for wants and needs.
2. Contact with people—to make new friends and spend time with other people.
3. Self esteem—to make one feel important and worthwhile.

Career goals are decisions you will make about the type of work you want to do. To set wise career goals, you will need to explore careers that are suitable to your values, interests, and talents.

Values are things that are important to you. Some values include:

1. Money: Will you need a lot of money to live the way you hope to live in the future? If so, you will want to research careers that pay well. If you plan to live modestly, this will not be a major value of influence.
2. Helping others: Do you like to help others? If you do, maybe you would like to research careers that involve helping other people.
3. Raising a family: Do you want to have children? If you want to raise a family and spend lots of time with them, you might have to check into careers that will not require you to work nights and/or weekends.
4. Having good health: Most people want to be healthy. Some jobs are more dangerous than others. Some jobs require the use of dangerous chemicals and equipment. You may want to evaluate health risks before you select a job.
5. Religion: If religious activities are important, you may not want to work on days that you attend religious services. You may also want to work in an area free of alcohol and profanity.

You must evaluate your values and select a career that supports your values.

Interests are the things you like to do. You need to explore your interests to select career choices that will be of interest to you. You learn about many subjects at school. What subjects are interesting to you? You may have hobbies that interest you. What are your hobbies? Many interest inventory tests are available through your school guidance counselor. These tests can give you a list of careers that match up with your interests. **Evaluate your interests and select career choices that support your interests.**

Talent is the ability to learn or perform a task easily. Your talents are the things you are good at doing. Your talents may be mental, physical, or social talents. It is a good idea to select a career choice that utilizes your talents. **Select careers that are realistic choices for the talents you possess.**

Mental talents are talents in areas such as math, science, reading, writing, or memory skills. Your grades will reflect your areas of mental talent.

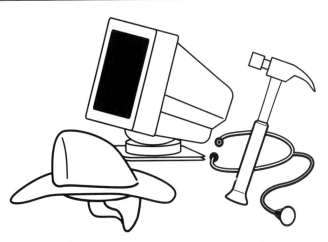

Physical talents are talents that require physical abilities, such as physical strength, finger dexterity, sports ability, musical ability, and artistic ability.

Social talents include the ability to work well with others. Some social talents are public speaking, understanding the needs of others, and motivating others.

Many careers require a combination of talents. Evaluate your areas of talent and select careers that utilize your talents.

Now you are aware of the areas that you should explore to make wise career choices for your future. Begin exploring the world of work and the vast number of careers that are available to you. Chances are, you will change your mind as you grow older. Select several careers that may be possibilities for the future. Be sure to consider your personal values, interests, and talents to select the careers that will be best for you.

Additional Activities:

1. Interview five people regarding their careers. Ask them how their present careers support their values, interests, and talents. Share your findings with the class.

2. Take a poll of 10 working adults. Ask them if they are working in the career that they projected they wanted when they were your age. Report your findings to your class. Discuss the implications of poll results.

3. Select a career that interests you. Make a poster that shows the values, interests, and talents that would be necessary for the career.

4. Research the necessary education for the career that you selected in the previous activity. Where could you receive the training that you will need for this career?

5. List the hobbies that you enjoy. List the possible careers that coincide with your hobbies.

6. Interview a person who is working in the career that you might like in the future. Ask them about job requirements, educational requirements, salary, benefits, hours of work per week, opportunities for advancement, and any other questions you may have. Write a short report summarizing your findings from the interview. Does this career still interest you?

7. Ask a person who is working in the career that interests you if you could job-shadow them for a day. **Job-shadowing** is the experience of visiting a person on the job and observing them as they perform their routine tasks. You may be able to perform some of the job tasks with them to gain experience and insight into the job. Report on your experience to the class.

Name: _____ Date: _____

For the Student

1. A career is _____

    _____

2. The three main reasons people work are:

    a. _____

    b. _____

    c. _____

3. Values are _____

    _____

4. List five values that might influence your career selection.

    a. _____

    b. _____

    c. _____

    d. _____

    e. _____

5. Which of these values is most important to you? Why?

    _____

    _____

6. List three of your areas of interest.

    a. _____

    b. _____

    c. _____

7. Talents are _____

    _____

8. List two examples of each of the following types of talents.

    Mental talent

    a. _____

    b. _____

    Physical talent

    a. _____

    b. _____

    Social talent

    a. _____

    b. _____

Name: _____ Date: _____

For the Student: Values

List three values that are important to you.

1. _____
2. _____
3. _____

List three jobs that would go against your values and state the reasons why.

1. _____
2. _____
3. _____

List three jobs that would support your values and state the reasons why.

1. _____
2. _____
3. _____

State something you would value about each of the categories below. An example is *Fame: I would like to be well-known in the town in which I live.*

1. Money: _____

2. Power: _____

3. Religion: _____

4. Serving others: _____

5. Family: _____

6. Health: _____

7. Art: _____

8. Creativity: _____

9. Social: _____

10. Time: _____

Name: _____ Date: _____

For the Student: Interests

Match each interest area with the job that relates to it.

_____ 1. Conservation Officer	A. Mathematics
_____ 2. Daycare Worker	B. Animals
_____ 3. Artist	C. Problem Solving
_____ 4. Veterinarian	D. Child Care
_____ 5. Stewardess	E. Marine Life
_____ 6. Musician	F. Mechanics
_____ 7. Counselor	G. Painting
_____ 8. Teacher	H. Decorating
_____ 9. Marine Biologist	I. Piano
_____ 10. Radio Broadcaster	J. Flowers
_____ 11. Interior Decorator	K. Teaching Children
_____ 12. Auto Mechanic	L. Wildlife
_____ 13. Chef	M. Computers
_____ 14. P.E. Teacher	N. Cooking
_____ 15. Librarian	O. Communications
_____ 16. Accountant	P. Books
_____ 17. Beautician	Q. Sports
_____ 18. Computer Programmer	R. Hair Styling
_____ 19. Secretary	S. Travel
_____ 20. Florist	T. Office Skills

Name: _____ Date: _____

For the Student: Talents

List three jobs that would support talents in the following areas.

Creative Writing

1._____
2._____
3._____

Vocal Music

1._____
2._____
3._____

Photography

1._____
2._____
3._____

Caring for others

1._____
2._____
3._____

Mathematics

1._____
2._____
3._____

Computers

1._____
2._____
3._____

Athletics

1._____
2._____
3._____

Public Speaking

1._____
2._____
3._____

Name: _____ Date: _____

For the Student: Choosing a Career

Now that you have explored your values, interests, and talents, you may have some ideas about which careers might be suitable for you. Answer each of the following questions to help you select a suitable career.

1. What values are important to you? _____

_____.

2. List your interests. _____

3. List your talents. _____

4. Do you want to attend college?_____ Where? _____

5. Where would you like to live in the future? _____

6. Would you like to marry and have a family? _____

7. What hours would you like to work? _____

8. Would you like to work on weekends? _____

9. Would you like to have summers off? _____

10. What type of setting would you like to work in? (school, office, etc.) _____

11. Would you like to do the same work every day? _____

12. Would you like to be responsible for other employees?_____

13. Would you like to help other people? _____

14. Would you like to work alone or with a group? _____

15. How much money would you like to earn per year? _____

16. Would you like to have the freedom to be creative in your career? _____

17. List three careers that would be suitable for you. _____

_____

18. List part-time jobs that would provide experience for each of the career choices above.

_____

_____

Getting a Job

You will probably have many different jobs in your lifetime. You need to develop skills and a plan to help you get the jobs you want. You need to know how to find available jobs, apply for a job, write a resume, and interview for a job. The following information and activities will help you develop employment skills to get the jobs you want.

Finding a job: Some sources of finding available jobs include:

1. Your family and friends: Ask friends and family members if their places of employment are hiring. It helps to have someone put in a good word for you with the person doing the hiring.
2. Your school: Your counselor or work program coordinator may know of jobs available in your community. Your teachers would be a good source for recommendations.
3. Newspaper ads: Read the Help Wanted ads in your local newspaper to find jobs available in your area. Check them regularly because new positions are added daily.
4. Employment agencies: Some towns have local or government employment agencies. These agencies may or may not charge a fee to help you obtain employment. Ask about fees before you obtain their services.

Applying for a job: Most businesses that have jobs available will ask you to fill out a job application. If you fill out the application neatly and correctly, you will have a better chance of getting the job. You may be allowed to take the application home to complete, or you may be required to complete it on the spot. Some tips to help you are listed below.

1. Use a pen.
2. Print the information neatly.
3. Follow directions.
4. Answer every question.
5. Spell correctly.
6. List all of your qualifications for the job.
7. Be honest and truthful with your answers.
8. For references, list people who will give you good recommendations.
9. List all of your previous work experience.

Preparing a resume: A **resume** is a summary of facts about you that might be of interest to an employer. Some places of employment will ask you for your resume when you attend an interview. A resume should be typed neatly and include the following:

1. Your complete name, address, and telephone number.
2. Your skills. List the skills that are related to the position you are applying for.
3. Educational background. Include high school and college information.
4. Work experience. List all past job titles, dates of employment, job duties, employer names, addresses, and phone numbers. List your most recent job first and your first job last.
5. Personal information. Include date of birth, interests, hobbies, and honors.
6. References. List three or four people who will give you a good recommendation. List their names, addresses, and phone numbers. Ask the people if you may use them as a reference before you place them on your resume.

Interviewing for a job: An interview is your opportunity to show the employer that you are the best person for this job. You need to make a good impression. Some tips to follow for a successful interview are:

1. Be well-groomed. Make sure your body, hair, and nails appear neat and clean. Dress appropriately and neatly. Wear clothing that would be appropriate for the job you are applying for.
2. Arrive for the interview at least five minutes early. Ask for directions if you are unsure about where you are going.
3. Use proper grammar. Speak clearly and use good grammar. Write using correct grammar and spelling.
4. Be polite and businesslike. Introduce yourself to the interviewer. Use good manners and show respect for the interviewer. Do not chew gum or smoke during the interview. Answer questions honestly. Maintain eye contact with the interviewer. Be prepared to ask questions that indicate your interest in the position available. Thank the interviewer for giving you the opportunity to interview.
5. Write a thank-you letter to the interviewer for the interview. Indicate your continued interest in the position.

Try to perfect your employment skills to help you get the job you want!

Additional Activities:

1. Use your local newspaper's Help Wanted ads to locate three jobs that interest you. Discuss your choices with the class.

2. Gather two sample job applications from local businesses. Fill them out neatly and correctly.

3. Prepare a sample resume.

4. Practice mock interviews. Discuss ways to improve your interviewing techniques.

5. Come to school dressed for an interview for a job that you secretly chose. Ask the class to guess what type of job you will be interviewing for. Discuss whether your clothes were appropriate for the job that you chose.

6. Have local employment agencies give a presentation to the class regarding the services that they provide.

7. Ask an interviewer for a local business to tell the class what he or she looks for when interviewing potential employees.

8. Write a thank-you letter to an interviewer.

Name: _____ Date: _____

For the Student

1. List four sources of finding available jobs.

   a. _____

   b. _____

   c. _____

   d. _____

2. List seven tips for filling out a job application properly.

   a. _____

   b. _____

   c. _____

   d. _____

   e. _____

   f. _____

   g. _____

3. A resume is

   _____

   _____

4. List six items that should be included in your resume.

   a. _____

   b. _____

   c. _____

   d. _____

   e. _____

   f. _____

5. List five tips to follow for a successful interview.

   a. _____

   b. _____

   c. _____

   d. _____

   e. _____

Name: _____ Date: _____

For the Student: True or False

Place a T in the blank if the statement is true and an F in the blank if it is false.

_____ 1. You may chew gum during an interview.

_____ 2. Most people have only one job in their lifetime.

_____ 3. List all of your previous job experiences on the job application.

_____ 4. Wear wrinkled clothing to the interview.

_____ 5. Fill out the job application in pencil.

_____ 6. You may wear neat jeans to an interview for a job as a landscaper.

_____ 7. Lie about your job experience on the application.

_____ 8. You may wear tennis shoes to an interview for a secretarial position.

_____ 9. Find jobs available on the social page of the newspaper.

_____ 10. Write your nickname on the resume.

_____ 11. Treat the interviewer with respect.

_____ 12. You may handwrite your resume.

_____ 13. Write the job application in cursive.

_____ 14. Arrive thirty minutes early for your interview.

_____ 15. Ask your friends and family if they know about any available jobs.

_____ 16. Write a thank-you letter to the interviewer following your interview.

_____ 17. You may use slang during your interview.

_____ 18. Fill out every question on the job application and draw a line if it does not apply to you.

_____ 19. You should avoid eye contact with the interviewer.

_____ 20. List references that will give you a good recommendation.

Being a Good Employee

Getting a job is an important achievement in your life. Each job has specific duties and rules to follow. You will be proud of your new job, and you want to be a good employee. If you are not a good worker, you will lose your job. Good employees get promotions and raises!

Tips to Being a Good Employee

1. Display a positive attitude. Be friendly and pleasant.

2. Work fast, but do a good job. Do not waste time.

3. Finish each task that is assigned to you correctly. Be a hard worker. Be proud of your work.

4. Use your employer's time fairly. Arrive at work on time. Take only assigned breaks. Never leave your job early.

5. Follow the established rules. Each employer has specific rules about work, eating, dress, cleanliness, and so on. Learn the rules and follow them.

6. Always be well groomed and dress appropriately for your job.

7. Always follow safety rules and regulations.

8. Be cooperative. Try to get along with your fellow employees and customers.

9. Be dependable. Being dependable means that your coworkers can count on you to do your job. If you must be absent from work, follow the correct procedure to inform your employer. Catch up on work you missed as soon as possible upon returning to work.

10. Show initiative. **Initiative** is doing the work that needs to be done without being told. Look around and find work to keep busy. Be a self-starter!

11. Be eager to learn and be enthusiastic about your job.

12. Display loyalty to your employer. Do not discuss confidential information. Do not speak badly about your employer.

13. Be honest. Do not steal time or materials from your employer.

14. Accept criticism and be willing to make changes to improve your work.

15. Be polite and treat others with the respect that you would desire.

Name: _____ Date: _____

For the Student : True or False

Place a T in the blank if the statement is true and an F in the blank if it is false.

_____ 1. You may discuss confidential information concerning your job with your friends.

_____ 2. Always be well-groomed for your job.

_____ 3. Each job has the same duties and rules to follow.

_____ 4. Always follow safety rules and regulations.

_____ 5. Try to get along with all of your coworkers.

_____ 6. Display a positive attitude.

_____ 7. Accept criticism and make changes to improve your work.

_____ 8. Take extra coffee breaks if you are having a bad day.

_____ 9. It is all right to take office supplies home with you from work.

_____ 10. If you are not a good worker, you will probably lose your job.

_____ 11. Treat others with the respect you desire.

_____ 12. You can break the dress code if you do not feel like getting dressed up.

_____ 13. Arrive to work 10 minutes late every day.

_____ 14. Rules are made to be broken.

_____ 15. Work slowly and do a good job.

_____ 16. Bad employees get promotions and pay raises.

_____ 17. Be a self-starter.

_____ 18. Make your boss tell you each job that he or she wants you to do.

_____ 19. Talk bad about your employer to anyone who will listen.

_____ 20. Try to be negative about your job and coworkers.

Answer Keys

Understanding Yourself (page 2)
1. Unique means no other person is just like you. Appearance, personality, and skills are different.
2. Personality is the total of all the behavioral qualities that make up an individual.
3. Traits are qualities that make you different.
4. kind, moody, nice, confident, friendly, depressed, sloppy, happy, funny, excitable, etc.
5. Self-analysis is understanding who you are.
6. Self-concept is how you feel about yourself.
7. kind, friendly, nice, responsible, happy, etc.
8. sloppy, moody, mean, rude, lazy, etc.

Setting Goals (page 6)
1. A goal is something you want to accomplish.
2. a goal you accomplish in a short time
3. clean your room, buy a bike, pass a test, etc.
4. a goal you accomplish in a long time
5. graduate from college, raise a family, get a job, etc.
6. What are you going to do? How are you going to do it? When are you going to do it?
7–10. Answers will vary.

Communicating (pages 12–13)
1. The exchange of information (send/receive).
2a. Verbal: use of words to send information. Examples are speaking, writing, listening, etc.
b. Nonverbal: any means of sending a message that does not use words. Examples are body language, appearance, and posture.
3. pay attention, act interested, maintain eye contact, be patient, stay focused, ask questions, listen to the way the speaker uses his/her voice.
4. keeps messages short and to the point, considerate to others, respects the listener, uses language and pronunciation clearly, uses voice to emphasize message, maintains eye-contact
5. reading the newspaper, reading street signs, reading recipes.
6. writing a letter, answering questions on a test, writing a check
7. Body language is sending messages through body movements such as facial expressions, gestures, posture, appearance, and manners.
8. Caring for your body, clothes, hair, teeth, and nails
9. slumping, frowning, thumbs down, grimacing
10. smile, wave, thumbs up, good manners

11.
a. -	f. -	k. +	p. +	u. +
b. +	g. -	l. +	q. +	v. -
c. +	h. -	m. +	r. +	w. -
d. +	i. +	n. -	s. +	x. +
e. +	j. -	o. +	t. -	y. -

Relationships (page 15)
1. a person you have met, but do not know well
2. school, work, neighborhood, etc.
3. people you know who share the same interests and activities that you do
4. speech class, baseball team, drama club, etc.
5. your best friends, you spend most of your time with this group of people
6. loyal, caring, honest, reliable, funny, nice, etc.
7–8. Answers will vary.

Family (pages 18–19)
1. k - single parent 　d - family
　 i - beginning stage 　j - aging stage
　 h - extended family 　a - nuclear family
　 e - developing stage 　c - launching stage
　 g - family life cycle 　f - blended family
　 b - expanding stage
2a. blended, b. nuclear, c. extended, d. single-parent
3. various answers
4. spend time together, communicate with them, show appreciation and respect, share values and beliefs, resolve conflicts
5. various answers
6a. a newly-married couple
　 b. a couple with pre-school aged children
　 c. a couple with children in school
　 d. children in school and college
　 e. a retired couple
7–10. various answers

Caring for Children (page 22)
1. use straps on high chairs/strollers, use gates on stairways, keep screens on windows, use a playpen, cover electrical outlets, keep hot things out of reach, keep plastic bags away from small children, etc.
2. phone number where parents can be reached, emergency numbers, address and phone number of the house you are sitting at, phone number of a relative if parents cannot be reached.
3. keep the children safe and free from danger
4. various answers
5. emergency lists, rules for snacks, bed, etc.
6. various answers
7. reliable, follows parents' directions, writes down phone messages, plays with children, is a good role model, etc.
8. being kind, polite, using good language, being honest, neat, etc.

Caring for the Elderly (page 24)
1. wrinkling skin, changes in hair color, hearing loss, changes in posture, vision changes, arthritis, dental problems, forgetting, etc.

2. speak loudly and clearly, get devices to amplify sound, look at who you are speaking to, etc.

3. obtain large print materials, add additional lighting, read to the person, etc.

4. grandchildren, time to travel, retirement, etc.
   bad health, death of friends, less income, etc.

5–6. various answers

7. nursing home, owning a home, retirement home, living with relatives, etc.

8. various answers

Consumer Skills (page 26)

1. a spending plan to help you manage money
2. It provides you with items wanted and needed.
3. It can be upsetting if you do not have enough money to meet your needs and wants.
4. needs: food, clothes, shelter, medicine, etc.
wants: vacations, new TV, bigger house, etc.
5–7. various answers
8. fixed: insurance, loan and house payment
flexible: food, clothes, recreation
9. to establish a good savings routine

Advertising Activity (pages 31–32)

lettuce	$1.98	$1.52	$0.46
spaghetti	0.99	0.75	0.24
pork chops	5.98	3.38	2.60
biscuits	0.90	0.75	0.15
spag. sauce	3.96	3.00	0.96
milk	2.19	1.79	0.40
hamburger	3.38	1.98	1.40
cake mix	2.18	1.78	0.40
frosting	2.58	1.98	0.60
eggs	1.96	1.52	0.44
pizza	7.77	5.07	2.70
mac & cheese	0.96	0.67	0.29
buns	1.00	0.50	0.50
gelatin	0.99	0.75	0.24
soda	6.39	4.99	1.40
		TOTAL SAVED	$12.78

Reading Labels (page 33)

1. size 12
2. polyester, cotton
3. machine wash, tumble dry
4. That Girl
5. Island Sweet
6. sliced pineapple in pineapple juice
7. 20 oz.
8. sliced pineapple, pineapple juice
9. 2 slices
10. about 5
11. 60
12. total fat grams - 0 g   % daily value 0%

13. cholesterol grams - 0 mg   % daily value 0%
14. sodium grams - 10 mg   % daily value 0%
15. tot. carbohydrates - 16 g   % daily value 5%
16. protein - 0 g   % daily value 0%
17. Vitamin A - 0 g   % daily value 0%
18. Dietary fiber - 1 g   % daily value 4%
19. Iron - Not Available   % daily value 2%
20. Vitamin C - NA   % daily value 20%

Food Pyramid Grouping Activity (page 36)

Milk: butter, American cheese, yogurt, cream, milk shake, chocolate milk, cottage cheese, ice cream, skim milk, pudding

Vegetable: french fries, asparagus, cauliflower, tossed salad, corn, broccoli, carrots, potatoes, peas

Meat: turkey, peanut butter, pork chop, chicken, egg, liver, beefsteak, tuna, hamburger, cashews

Fruit: apple, applesauce, bananas, pears, peach, cherry pie, watermelon, cranberry juice, orange juice, raisins

Bread: macaroni, hamburger bun, cornflakes, rice, pancakes, oatmeal, crackers, muffins, biscuits

USDA Dietary Guidelines (page 38)

1. Use the Food Guide Pyramid to select a variety of foods from the various food groups.
2. Exercise daily to use up the calories provided by the food.
3. Eat pasta, breads, cereals, and vegetables, which are low fat and high in vitamins, minerals, carbos, and fiber, instead of meats, fats, and sugars.
4. Eat less food from milk and meat groups, eat few fried foods, more fruits and vegetables.
5. Select foods that are low in sugar or are sugar-free.
6. Purchase low or no sodium varieties of foods, and reduce the amount of table salt you use.
7. Limit the days and amounts you drink.

Nutrients (page 41)

1. the chemicals in food to keep you healthy and fit
2. following the Food Guide Pyramid recommendations.
3. energy; fiber; digestion; sugars; starches; fruits/vegetables/honey/grains/pasta
4. energy; flavor; butter/margarine/cheese/meat/ice cream/nuts/milk; overweight/obese
5. build; repair; systems; energy; meats/eggs/dried beans/fish/poultry/milk/peanut butter
6. skin; night blindness; resist; liver/dark green vegetables/yellow fruits and vegetables/milk/egg yolks
7. riboflavin; thiamin; niacin; skin; nervous system; liver/meat/eggs/poultry/whole grains/milk/dark green leafy vegetables
8. bones; teeth; gums; infection; wounds; citrus fruits/broccoli/canteloupe/strawberries/cabbage/potatoes

9. bones; teeth; fish oil/ fortified milk; sunlight

10. bones; teeth; clot; heart; nerves; muscles; milk/ dairy products/green leafy vegetables/sardines

11. cells; oxygen; liver/meat/egg yolk/dried fruit/beans/ dark green leafy vegetables/enriched breads/cereals; anemia

12. salt; water; blood pressure

Meal Appeal (page 44)

Color - orange juice, eggs, toast, bacon, grits.

Flavors - spicy: pizza, tacos, barbecue sauce, etc.
  sweet: candy, soda, ice cream, etc.
  sour: lemon, dill pickle, etc.
  bland: mashed potato, rice, etc.

Shapes - sandwich (square), potato chips (round), peaches (wedges), cake (square), etc.

Texture - crunchy: cereal, raw vegetables, apples, etc.
  sticky: peanut butter, honey, syrup, jelly, etc.
  soft: ice cream, milk shake, gelatin, pudding, etc.
  chewy: caramel, steak, crisped rice treats, pork chops, etc.

Temperature - tossed salad, steak, corn on the cob, ice cream (various answers)

Healthy Snacking (page 45)

Milk Group - pudding, ice cream bar, yogurt, cheese, etc.

Meat Group - peanuts, peanut butter sandwich, deviled eggs, beef jerky, etc.

Vegetable Group - raw vegetables (with dip), potato skins, etc.

Fruit Group: raisins, apple, orange, fruits and dip, etc.

Bread Group - bagel, crackers and cheese, pretzels, cereal, etc.

Calories (page 47)

1. a scientific unit of measure that indicates energy released from the burning of food in the body

2. energy and to keep your body warm

3. If you consume more calories than you burn, you gain. If you consume less calories, you lose.

4. age, sex, body size, activity level

5. various answers

6. No, they should eat less.

7. various answers

8. 30 percent or less

9. read labels, calorie guide books

10. carrot sticks, celery sticks, diet soda, water, low-fat yogurt, banana, apple, lettuce, sugar-free gelatin, sugar-free cereals, etc.

Exercise (page 50)

1. 160–240   3 hours
   80–100   6 hours
   240–350   2 hours
   350–500   2 hours
   100–160   4 hours

2. strengthens muscles, builds endurance, reduces disease risk, improves appearance, improves posture, helps relaxation, controls weight, develops self-esteem, etc.

3–4. various answers

Drugs and Alcohol (pages 53–54)

1. peer pressure, escape reality, act grown-up

2. The body becomes dependent on the substance and it craves the continued use.

3. colorless, odorless drug, gives the body a lift

4. causes cancers, heart and lung disease, discolors teeth, bad breath, women who smoke during pregnancy have low birth weight babies

5. Passive smoke is the smoke that non-smokers breathe when others around them smoke. Banning smoking and creating smoking areas reduces the dangers of passive smoke.

6. classes, special gum, nicotine patches

7. It slows activity in brain and body reflexes.

8. It is the disease caused by dependence on alcohol. It can be treated, but is hard to cure.

9. slows brain activity, slows reflexes, slurred speech, lack of muscle control

10. damages liver, stomach, esophagus, brain, heart

11. They impair reflexes and cause drivers to drive erratically and have accidents.

12. legal: pain pills, diet pills, inhalants, etc.
    illegal: marijuana, cocaine, crack, etc.

13. lung/liver damage, prone to infection, memory loss, emotional problems, seizures, etc.

14. The people under the influence of drugs and alcohol have difficulty holding jobs and will do anything to get alcohol or drugs. They behave erratically and may become violent when under the influence of drugs or alcohol.

15. various answers

Kitchen Measurement (page 57)

1. Dry measuring cups; flour, sugars, butter, etc.

2. liquid measuring cup; milk, water, oil, juice, etc.; flat surface; eye level

3. small; 1 tablespoon, 1 teaspoon, $\frac{1}{2}$ teaspoon, $\frac{1}{4}$ teaspoon; plastic or metal; ring

4. packed; dry; leveled off

5. Butter; margarine; shortening; exact

6. White; before; waxed paper; gently; dry measuring cup; level; knife; air; lumps

7. teaspoon - t./tsp.   ounce - oz.
   tablespoon - T./Tbsp.   pint - pt.
   cup - c.   quart - qt.
   pound - lb.   gallon - gal.

8. 3, 16, 2, 2, 4, 8, 16, 32, 128
9. terrible, etc.

Kitchen Safety (page 59)

1. T	5. F	9. T	13. F	17. T
2. T	6. F	10. T	14. F	18. T
3. T	7. F	11. T	15. F	19. F
4. F	8. F	12. T	16. T	20. F

Food Storage & Kitchen Cleanliness (pages 61–62)

1. F	6. T	11. F	16. T	21. T	26. F
2. F	7. F	12. F	17. T	22. T	27. F
3. T	8. F	13. T	18. T	23. F	28. T
4. F	9. F	14. T	19. F	24. T	29. T
5. F	10. T	15. F	20. T	25. T	30. F

1. b   2. c

Table Manners (page 64)

1. rules or guidelines for eating politely
2. so others will enjoy eating with you

3. T	7. F	11. T	15. T	19. T
4. F	8. F	12. F	16. F	20. F
5. F	9. F	13. T	17. T	
6. T	10. T	14. F	18. F	

Table Settings (page 66)

1. silverware on wrong sides of plate, fork on top of napkin, knife blade facing out instead of in, glass on wrong side
2. fork on top of napkin, cup in wrong place
3.

4.

Your Grooming Routine (page 73)

1. care; trying; best
2. body, hair, teeth, hands, clothing
3. daily; soap, water; perspiration/dirt
4. Perspiration; body odor

5. deodorant, antiperspirant
6. more; sports
7. Shaving
8. normal, oily, dry, or combination
9. Oily
10. Dry
11. dermatologist
12. T-zone
13. Sun; sunscreen
14. meal; snack
15. floss; plaque/tartar
16. once, twice
17. manicure; pedicure
18. oil, dirt, dead skin
19. hair cut/style; lifestyle

Exploring Careers (page 80)

1. work or job people do for a number of years
2. money, contact with people, self-esteem
3. things that are important to you
4. money, helping, family, health, religion
5–6. various answers
7. ability to learn/perform tasks–things you're good at
8. mental: math, science, reading, writing, etc.
physical: basketball, running, typing, painting, etc.
social: public speaking, motivating, counseling, etc.

Interests (page 82)

1. L	5. S	9. E	13. N	17. R
2. D	6. I	10. O	14. Q	18. M
3. G	7. C	11. H	15. P	19. T
4. B	8. K	12. F	16. A	20. J

Getting a Job (page 87)

1. family, friends, school, newspaper, agencies
2. use pen, print neatly, follow directions, answer all questions, spelling, honesty, good references, list all previous work experience, etc.
3. facts about you that might interest employer
4. name, address, phone number, skills, education, work experience, personal info, references
5. well-groomed, five minutes early, grammar, polite, businesslike, write a thank-you letter

Getting a Job: True or False (page 88)

1. F	5. F	9. F	13. F	17. F
2. F	6. T	10. F	14. F	18. T
3. T	7. F	11. T	15. T	19. F
4. F	8. F	12. F	16. T	20. T

Being a Good Employee: True or False (page 90)

1. F	5. T	9. F	13. F	17. T
2. T	6. T	10. T	14. F	18. F
3. F	7. T	11. T	15. F	19. F
4. T	8. F	12. F	16. F	20. F